MAJOR DISASTERS
OF THE WORLD

Herbert Genzmer
Sybille Kershner
Christian Schütz

Parragon

Bath New York Singapore Hong Kong Cologne Delhi Melbourne

Copyright © Parragon Books Ltd 2007

Parragon Books Ltd
Queen Street House
4 Queen Street
Bath BA1 1 HE, UK

Original edition production: ditter.projektagentur GmbH
Project coordination: Irina Ditter-Hilkens
Texts:
  Herbert Genzmer: 5, 12–21, 26–29, 48–59, 68–71, 84–95
  Sybille Kershner: 6–11, 34–39
  Christian Schütz: 22–25, 30–33, 40–47, 60–67, 72–83
Picture research: Claudia Bettray
Design and layout: Claudio Martinez

English edition produced by: APE Int'l, Richmond, VA
Translation from German: Russell Cennydd and
  Markus Flatscher for APE Int'l
Editing of English edition: Dr. Pippin Michelli for APE Int'l

ISBN: 978-1-4075-0190-1

Printed in China

CONTENTS

PREFACE

Literally translated, the Greek word *katastraphei* (catastrophe) means either "turning away" or "calamity, doom, collapse." That is how the word catastrophe is understood today – as a disaster, a sudden turn of misfortune – thus lending credence to the belief that we live in a state of peace and security, and that calamity is something that suddenly and unexpectedly hits us, wreaking havoc when we least expect it. That is not entirely true, though. In this age so rich in disasters, calamity is a constant presence, even if we are fortunate enough not to have experienced it for ourselves or suffered its effects directly.

A book about disasters could be much thicker and heavier than this volume, even if it was limited to those that have afflicted (and continue to afflict) humanity since the beginning of the last century. Volcanoes and earthquakes have occurred since the beginning of time; storms and floods devastate parts of the world and claim their victims as never before; starvation and drought are our constant companions; diseases and epidemics have always accompanied humankind, and now diseases long thought to be cured have made threatening comebacks; war and terror are being waged in many places even as we write; horrors in the air and at sea, and the problems of world travel, are daily events. Finally, there is the curse of technology. While providing the Western world with all its creature comforts, it simultaneously demands its price and threatens us with fateful consequences.

In fact, disasters that occurred long ago would also have to be included: our planet is fragile and its history is rich in dramatic and often momentous events that shaped its structure long before humans appeared on the stage. Since our appearance, however, we have increasingly contributed to these events; indeed, most are now a direct consequence of our existence. Ever since the media has been able to report live throughout the world, recording and processing every event, these questions have come to the fore: how do people, how does one person, respond to a disaster? How can anyone handle the flood of catastrophic news that engulfs us daily? How can the scale of a disaster be measured? By counting the number of deaths it causes, or the tears of the bereaved and the survivors? Or would it be better to calculate the years that humanity or a group of people have been thrown back in their development? Damage can always be measured monetarily; insurance companies can provide exact data in this respect. But none of these are the true benchmark: it is the surprise, the occurrence of the unexpected. The yardstick is the inconceivable horror of the shock.

The selection of disasters presented in this book is largely based on this benchmark. What is the worst possible disaster? A tsunami? A dam burst? The in-flight collision of two jumbo jets? An atomic meltdown? All these horror scenarios have already happened to some degree, and have been presented to us live, but we assume that nothing so iniquitous could ever befall us personally. This is the only way people can continue living their lives. Events will always catch us unawares, no matter how carefully we try to prepare ourselves for them. And when the event actually happens, it leaves us gasping for breath every time.

THE BLACK DEATH – STILL A THREAT

THE PLAGUE PAST AND PRESENT

The plague is the epitome of the deadly epidemic – it has killed millions upon millions of people. As recently as between 1896 and 1930, over 12 million people fell victim to the plague, and even today WHO (World Health Organization) estimates that it claims a world-wide death toll of some 2,000 people every year. The Congo is currently a plague hot spot; Algeria, Malawi and India have not been spared in recent years either. Even in North America, people still occasionally contract the plague through contact with infected domestic cats.

From flea to rat to human

The plague is caused by gut bacteria of the *Yersinia pestis* family, which can hardly be eliminated among rodents living in the wild. Sick rats can transmit the disease to humans via fleas or other parasites, and human-to-human infection is also possible. There are two main types of plague. Bubonic plague announces itself with a swelling of the lymph nodes, and pneumonic plague is frequently accompanied by pneumonia, dark sputum and subdermal haemorrhages – hence the name "Black Death". In the case of septicaemia plague, which is a consequence of pneumonic plague, the blood is infected. Without medical treatment, the mortality rate for bubonic plague is 60–80 per cent, and almost 100 per cent for pneumonic plague.

In 14th-century Florence, Italy, the Black Death led to piles of corpses, mass misery and barbarization – all depicted here by Giovanni Boccaccio.

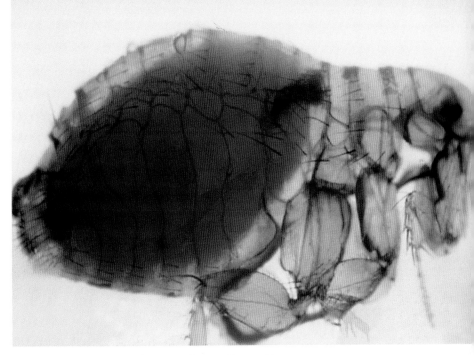

Rat fleas transmit plague bacteria; this is a flea on the third day of infection. The dark spot in its blood-filled stomach is a sign of the infection.

Early mass mortality

Early references to the plague include the Bible, which mentions the "diseases of Egypt" as a punishment meted out by God, and the Greek poet Homer, who described the rapid transmission of the plague (Greek *loimos* or *nosos*) metaphorically: Apollo and Artemis shoot Niobe's children with plague-tainted arrows (*Iliad*, Book 24). Ancient physicians would often take to their heels when confronted with epidemics, knowing that there was nothing they could do.

The first well-documented major plague epidemic occurred in Constantinople under Emperor Justinian (527–565). Probably introduced in 542 by ships coming from Egypt, it spread rapidly and claimed thousands of lives in many countries. Gregory of Tours (538/539–

A physician, protecting himself from the plague with an oilcloth gown and face mask. Sponges drenched in vinegar were also thought to prevent infection.

594), a well-known bishop and historian, was one of several who chronicled the disastrous consequences for France.

The Crusades add to the spreading

The epidemic flared up time and again, and the great armies regularly travelling across the continent during the Crusades only added to the problem. When the Seljuk Turks occupied Jerusalem, Christian pilgrims were no longer safe, and this led to Pope Urban II's call on Christendom to free Palestine. Urban offered the crusaders remission for their sins and eternal life. Of the 200,000 crusaders who set out on the First Crusade, only about 15,000 arrived in Jerusalem in 1099; the rest died on their way through infested areas; 50,000 are reported to have died in Antioch alone. The hospital ships that accompanied the knightly orders were a significant stimulus to the development of hospitals ashore.

The Black Death of 1347–1352

From 1325 to 1351, the plague ravaged China. Its agents proliferated in the fur of ship rats and in fur clothing, in particular. Originating from the Caspian Sea and Black Sea, the epidemic came to Venice and Messina via Constantinople and quickly reached every seaport town in the eastern Mediterranean. The *mortalega grande* (Great Mortality) had arrived. The consequences are described, for example, in Giovanni Boccaccio's famous collection of stories, *The Decameron*, written between 1348 and 1353. Boccaccio described how red-clad members of the *Compagnia della Misericordia* (Confraternity of Mercy) gathered up corpses with their long crooks, also scooping up the sick and dying to avoid having to come back for them

Patron saints
Many of the sick pray to patron saints, notably to St. Sebastian (died ca. 288), whose legend states that God brought him back from death after he was shot with arrows, and to St. Roch of Montpellier (ca. 1295–1327), who contracted the plague while caring for the sick but was saved by an angel and a dog who brought him bread.

This medieval representation of a plague patient from Anne of Britanny's Book of Hours shows the boils that are characteristic of the disease.

later. According to Boccaccio, from March 1348 until June 1349, over 100,000 people died in Florence alone. That same year, Siena lost half its population within a few months. Ships packed with plague patients were set adrift on the oceans. Some ships were driven out of Messina and landed in Marseille. From there, the plague spread to Avignon, the seat of the pope. Most of the 60,000 dead were thrown into the Rhône River because there were too few undertakers. While most physicians fled, the monastic orders, especially the Franciscans, cared for the sick. Frequently, those monks paid with their lives for practicing *caritas* (charity).

Moving north from Marseille in 1348, the Black Death reached Paris, then Calais, then England, whose population shrank from 4 million to 2.5 million. Almost all of Europe was in the clutch of the Black Death; only Poland and Russia had relatively large areas that remained unaffected. About a quarter of Europe's population, some 25 million people, perished of the plague. As a further consequence, the epidemic caused a mass emigration to the cities, with ensuing degeneration of farm land into steppe and resulting famines.

Early quarantine measures

Despite not knowing the mode of infection, the idea that the plague was contagious became increasingly prevalent, and hospitals were more often built outside city walls. Hygienic conditions (which were sometimes terrible) improved a little, and livestock breeding and muckheaps were restricted within the cities. Traditional treatment consisted in bloodletting, administering herbs and lancing the plague boils. Baths were avoided to prevent opening pores, which would make it easy for the disease to enter the body. The sick were quarantined, and rooms and belongings were fumigated with sulphur, saltpetre or camphor. Faces and hands were washed with vinegar and corpses were covered with lime. Many trading towns, especially Ragusa (now Dubrovnik) and Venice, forced potentially infected travellers to spend 30 days, and later 40 (*quaranta*), in quarantine. In Venice they had to stay in the Isola di S. Lazaro (St. Lazarus' Isle), where lepers traditionally had been quarantined – hence the term "to isolate". The *quaranta giorni*, on the other hand, have given their name to "quarantine".

Faith or prophylaxis?

In early modern times Constantinople (Istanbul) was a constant hotbed of the plague. The Turks trusted Allah with their lives and closed their quarantines. Many Christians subscribed to this fatalistic view as well and accepted their fate.

At the same time, provisions against the plague improved. People started burning plague victims' furniture and clothing, and the first attempt to study the "little worms" under a microscope was undertaken by the Jesuit priest Athanasius Kircher in 1656.

Although the *cordon sanitaire*, a military border 1,900 km (1,200 miles) long established by Austria to defend itself against Turkey, went a long way towards preventing further spreading of the plague by land, there were continued outbreaks. One was the Great Plague in London 1665–1666. The Great Plague of Marseille (1720–1722) was the last significant outbreak of plague in the Western world. The third pandemic, which originated in China during the second half of the nineteenth century, did not reach Europe.

In northern Namibia, DDT is sprayed to kill off plague fleas. While the pesticide is itself a health risk, it is less dangerous than the plague.

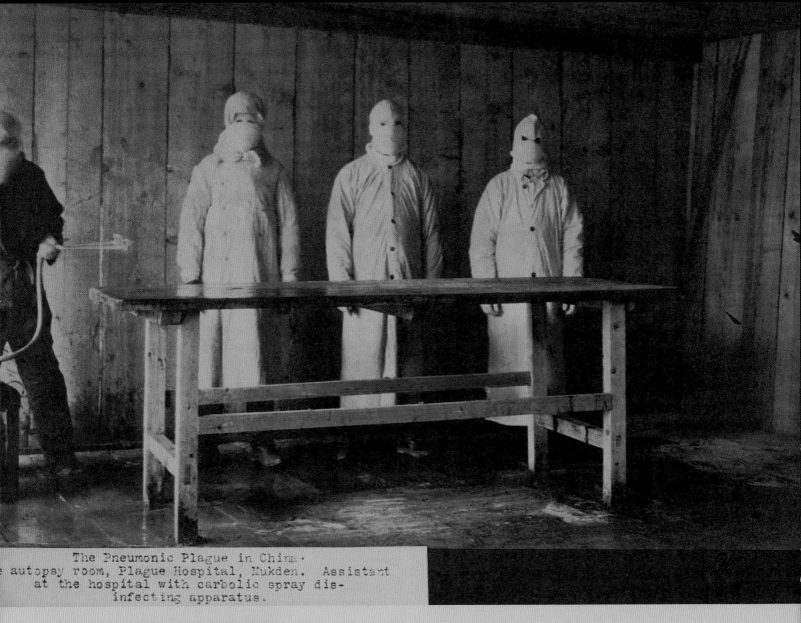

The Pneumonic Plague in China.
e autopsy room, Plague Hospital, Mukden. Assistant
at the hospital with carbolic spray dis-
infecting apparatus.

When the plague struck near Antananarivo, Madagascar in May 1983, all children had to stay indoors.

Today, the plague can be effectively treated with streptomycin, tetracycline and chloramphenicol. Nonetheless, further outbreaks cannot be avoided entirely, and sometimes there is no intention of avoiding them – on the contrary! Like the anthrax, smallpox and Ebola viruses, plague agents could be used for biological warfare, thus bringing back the horrors of medieval times.

An apparently sinister scene is actually an autopsy table being sprayed with disinfectant at the Mukden Plague Hospital in China during the winter of 1910/1911.

Covering the mouth with a hand

On August 29, 590, a city-wide church procession against the plague took place in Rome. Seven choirs marched simultaneously from seven different points of origin towards the church of Santa Maria Maggiore. It is said that 80 victims died of the plague en route, and this inevitably led to the infection of other participants. Since "pestilent" air was thought to be the cause of the disease at the time, this – according to legend – is the origin our habit of covering our mouth with a hand whenever we yawn or sneeze. But this had nothing to do with protection from airborne infection: it was to prevent demons from entering the body.

The Day the Sky Caught Fire

THE SAN FRANCISCO EARTHQUAKE OF 1906

At 5:13 a.m. on 18 April, 1906, San Francisco was hit by an earthquake of force 8.25 on the Richter scale, and then ravaged by the unquenchable four-day-long fire that ensued. Although the quake itself lasted hardly more than a minute, 490 city blocks containing some 25,000 buildings were destroyed. Of the city's roughly 400,000 inhabitants, 250,000 were made homeless, and more than 3,000 people were either killed by the quake or died in the flames.

The most devestating earthquake of all time

The San Francisco earthquake was one of the worst earthquakes of all time, and it put an abrupt end to the *belle epoque* of the golden city on the Pacific. A foreshock occurred along the San Andreas fault and throughout the Bay Area (the region around San Francisco Bay) at 5:12 a.m. on 18 April, 1906. The city was shaken within half a minute, as the epicenter lay just a short distance from the city limits. Shockwaves were felt from Oregon in the north to Los Angeles in the south and into Nevada. The city's various geological ground formations reacted in different ways to the earthquake: the greatest damage was suffered by the

Thick clouds of smoke darkened the sky above San Francisco.

areas of the city wrung from the bay through the process of land reclamation. In contrast to the rocky areas, the devastation here was total.

As powerful and damaging as it was, however, the earthquake itself was not responsible for the great devastation the city suffered, but the terrible fire triggered by it that so badly ravaged the city. The primary causes of the conflagration were short circuits on damaged power lines and escaping gas, but overturned heating stoves (mostly coal- or wood-fired) also started fires that could not be brought under control, especially since water mains had been broken by the quake. After the catastrophe, the number of fatalities officially reported was less than 700, but that figure has been corrected to something over 3,000, owing in part to the exclusion of the city's many inhabitants of Chinese descent.

Flames lit up the sky

Unimaginable panic erupted among the survivors of the quake as the fire took hold all around them with frightening speed, for it was not only the gas pipelines that had been damaged: the city's water supply had also been destroyed. The gas fed the flames and there was no water to put them out. In every quarter, helpers tried to bring in water to extinguish the burning houses, most of which were built of wood. Flames lit up the early morning sky, and by dawn an enormous pall of smoke, visible from afar, lay over the city.

Terrible tragedies took place in the devastated metropolis. Eyewitnesses reported three men on the roof of the burning Windsor Hotel on Market Street, for example, who could not possibly be rescued. To save them from being burned alive or leaping in desperation to certain death, the police officer responsible gave the order to shoot them. At another location, a man lay trapped under rubble as the fire approached. Helpers were unable to free him. As his feet began to burn, he begged to be put out of his misery. A police officer approached him, wrote down his personal details, and killed him with a shot to the head. Other tragedies occurred at the ferries, where tens of thousands of people attempted to escape the flames. Many more panic-stricken people fought their way onto ships than the ferries could possibly hold. On the same day, the mayor of the city at the time, E. E. Schmitz, gave the order that anyone caught looting or engaged in other criminal activity was to be shot.

The earthquake left behind destruction on an unbelievable scale – beautiful San Francisco lay in ruins.

Predicting the unpredictable

An earthquake is a convulsion on the earth's surface triggered by sudden activity in the earth's crust or upper mantle, primarily at geological faults. More than a million earthquakes occur each year, of which only very few, a handful at most, take on catastrophic dimensions. The Pacific Rim is an area with an especially high concentration of earthquakes. The San Andreas fault, responsible for the 1906 quake, is where the Pacific and North American continental plates meet. The fault stretches 1230 km (738 miles) through California, making it prone to further quakes. One of the world's best seismological institutes is located at the University of California at Berkeley, where scientists investigate earthquakes and endeavour to make exact predictions. A further great quake, "the Big One", is constantly being anticipated in San Francisco or Los Angeles, or at least preys on people's minds. Towards the end of 1980, a man entered a betting office in Las Vegas and wagered $5,000 that Los Angeles would be destroyed on New Year's Eve. He lost his bet. Nevertheless, the quakes happen – weekly, even daily – and they are felt all over the state. On 18 October 1989, an earthquake of magnitude 7.1 shook San Francisco, leading to 272 deaths and billions of dollars of damage. Just three years later, on

Market Street, almost completely destroyed, had been one of the city's most important arteries.

The city's wooden Victorian houses were almost all burnt down or so badly damaged that they had to be demolished.

28 June 1992, an earthquake of 7.4 that lasted 30 seconds occurred near Los Angeles. Almost a thousand aftershocks of up to 7.0 on the Richter scale followed. The damage "only" ran into the millions because the epicenter lay in the sparsely inhabited Mojave Desert.

Although it is still not possible for experts to foretell when an earthquake will take place, they can now predict accurately what will happen when one occurs at any given time. For example, it has been calculated that a quake in Los Angeles at 2 a.m.

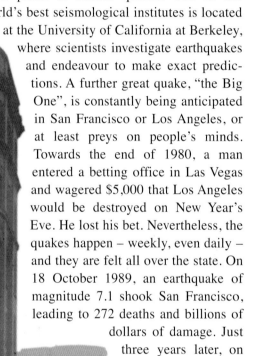

An urban freeway was almost completely destroyed by the quake of 1989.

would result in approximately 3,000 fatalities and 12,000 casualties, while a quake during the evening rush hour after 4:30 p.m. would claim some 23,000 lives and result in almost 100,000 injured. Los Angeles is spread over a much wider area with lower-built housing than San Francisco where, by contrast, the main causes of death and injury would be masonry falling from facades, collapsing buildings, and glass splinters raining down as windows burst.

Psychological effects

A doctor once wrote that one never gets used to earthquakes, and on the contrary, a kind of hypersensitivity is noticeable in most cases. Those who have been affected experience fear at the slightest vibration, even when it is only caused by a truck driving past. After a quake, many people refuse to sleep inside their houses, preferring to camp out in tents due to their fear of being buried under the rubble of a subsequent earthquake. It is not unusual for people to leave regions that have been hit by earthquakes and relocate entirely to locations they perceive as safer.

At the same time, however, earthquakes can also exercise a positive effect on the array of feelings people experience, namely when a kind of indifference or even arrogance sets in after surviving the catastrophe. The doctor mentioned above wrote that some individuals lose all their inhibitions, while others free themselves from unpleasant circumstances, gaining advantages for themselves and the circumstances of their lives from the worldly damage around them. Most survivors really do feel they have been given the gift of a new life. Others, wrote the Russian author Maxim Gorki in 1909, draw the conclusion that daily life and the so-called existential order is no more than a gigantic, slowly unfolding catastrophe, venting itself in occasional eruptions.

Bridges also collapsed in 1989 as if they were merely children's toys.

Predicting earthquakes

In the past, fluctuations in groundwater or electrical resistance, bulges in the earth's surface or abnormal animal behavior have all been considered indicators of earthquakes. This is all too unreliable for scientists. The reality is that predicting an earthquake precisely is very difficult, if not impossible. While it is possible to prognosticate a future earthquake, we cannot say when it will occur. The "Big Quake" has been expected in southern California (where two tectonic plates grate past each other by about 5 cm/2 in a year) for decades – but has not happened. To identify an imminent earthquake as early as possible, the hot spots of the San Andreas fault are scanned with lasers to register any seismic disturbance.

THE END OF A LUXURY LINER

THE SINKING OF THE TITANIC

On 14 April 1912 at 11:40 p.m., during her maiden voyage from Southampton to New York, the super liner *Titanic* collided with an iceberg southeast of Newfoundland. A mere 2 hours and 40 minutes later, the ocean liner disappeared under the surface of the North Atlantic Ocean. The sinking of the *Titanic* was the biggest nautical disaster prior to World War II. Of the 2,208 passengers and crew members on board, 1,504 perished.

Who has the speediest ship?

The RMS *Titanic* was part of American banker J.P. Morgan's White Star Line. She and her sister ships, the *Olympic*, which had passed her maiden voyage eight months earlier, and the *Gigantic* (later renamed *Britannic*), which was still being planned at the time of the great tragedy, were intended to take turns plying the route between Southampton, Cherbourg, France and New York City. All three of these top-of-the-line steamships were classified as RMS (Royal Mail Ships) and could thus transport mail. The contracts with Royal Mail offered additional profit for the shipping company.

The Titanic leaving Southampton on her maiden voyage into disaster. Eleven months earlier, she had been launched from Belfast docks, Ireland.

Until World War I, the great international shipping companies, mirroring the arms race taking place on the national level, were engaged in fierce competition as to who owned the fastest and most magnificent ship. The three ship designers who created the *Titanic* designed her not to be the fastest ship, but rather to be the biggest, safest and, above all, the most luxurious ship afloat. The press applauded the ship as a technological miracle and her safety equipment as the world's most advanced: the *Titanic* was considered unsinkable.

The most oppulent first class in the world

The steam liner's launch took place on 31 May 1911 in Belfast. In the year prior to her maiden voyage, construction of the interior and the furnishing and decoration progressed at high speed. The ship was registered with British authorities for a total capacity of 3,300 passengers, not including the crew. Because of the luxurious and spacious interiors of the first class cabins, however, the *Titanic* actually only had room for 2,400 passengers, 750 of whom could travel first class. These figures show the privileged status of first class accommodation aboard the *Titanic*. The super liner not only offered spacious suites, but also amenities including a squash court, an onboard swimming pool, splendid smoking and dining halls, libraries, cafés, a promenade deck and private decks that belonged to the suites. Second class accommodations on the *Titanic* offered the same level of comfort as the first class sections of older ships. Even in third class, the *Titanic* set new standards: where other ships had previously had large dormitories, the *Titanic* had passenger cabins for four, with one double bed and a set of bunk beds. The voyage was intended to be comfortable even for second and third class passengers, not least because emigrants to America were the most secure source of income for the White Star Line. Rates for a third class cabin started at $36, and second class rooms were available from $60.

Only half booked for her maiden voyage

At the beginning of the nineteenth century, a maiden voyage was considered a great social event, and thus many passengers aboard the

Chief Purser Hugh Walter McElroy (left) and Captain Edward J. Smith on the Titanic.

Technical specs for the Titanic

Ship type: passenger steamer
Class: Olympic
Purpose: transatlantic liner
Capacity: 46,329 GRT
Displacement: 53,147 tons
Length: 269.04 m/882 ft 9 in
Beam: 28.19 m/92 ft 6 in
Draft (at 52,310 long tons):
  10.54 m/34 ft 7 in
Height (keel to rim of funnel):
  56 m/183 ft 8 in
Propulsion and engines: three
propellers, two four-cylinder piston steam engines, one low-pressure Parsons turbine
Power: 51,000 hp/38 MW (registered)
Speed: 21 knots (ca. 24 mph)
Consumption: 6,700 tons coal storage capacity; daily consumption ca. 630 tons
Number of passengers: First Class: 750, Second Class: 550, Third Class: 1,100
Crew: 897
Construction cost: £1.5 million (over £90 million in today's currency)

Even so, the majestic liner was only a little more than half booked for her maiden sailing. Many people had decided against a trip on the *Titanic* because of a coal industry strike, with the result that a mere 1,311 passengers were on board the "largest ship in the world," as she was billed in advertisements, plus 897 crew members. Of those, 500 tended to the passengers while the rest took care of running the ship.

Accompanied by great fanfare and the sound of orchestras playing – no expense was spared on the occasion of her send-off – the *Titanic* left Southampton on 10 April 1912, a legend even before her first voyage.

Apparent post-collision stability

Only four days after her departure, around 11:40 p.m., the *Titanic*'s maiden voyage came to an abrupt end when the lookouts identified an iceberg directly ahead, and consequently rang the alarm bell three times. Meanwhile, an officer on duty had already spotted the iceberg himself and had initiated an evasive maneuver. This failed, however, because the *Titanic* was already too close to change its course. At undiminished cruise speed, the ocean liner's starboard side hit the sharp-edged block of ice. One of the firefighters on board would later liken the sound of the collision to the sound of cotton being torn apart. The consequences of the impact were severe; ice-cold water began to pour into the hull. Initially, the foundering could be slowed down by pumps working at full speed, but even so, during the first hour alone approximately 25,000 tons of water burst into the ship.

In addition to the decks and storage rooms, this cutaway shows the probable spot where the iceberg breached the Titanic.

Titanic were not really travellers. People whose primary interest was in crossing the Atlantic generally travelled in second and third class, while the deluxe suites, priced at $4,350, were booked for the pleasure of participating in history by many of the rich and famous of European and American high society. Among these, the list of distinguished passengers included Isidor Strauss, owner of Macy's department store in New York City; multimillionaire John Jacob Astor IV; writer Jacques Futrelle; Texan oil millionaire Margaret Brown; American actress Dorothy Gibson; and John B. Thayer, the railway magnate.

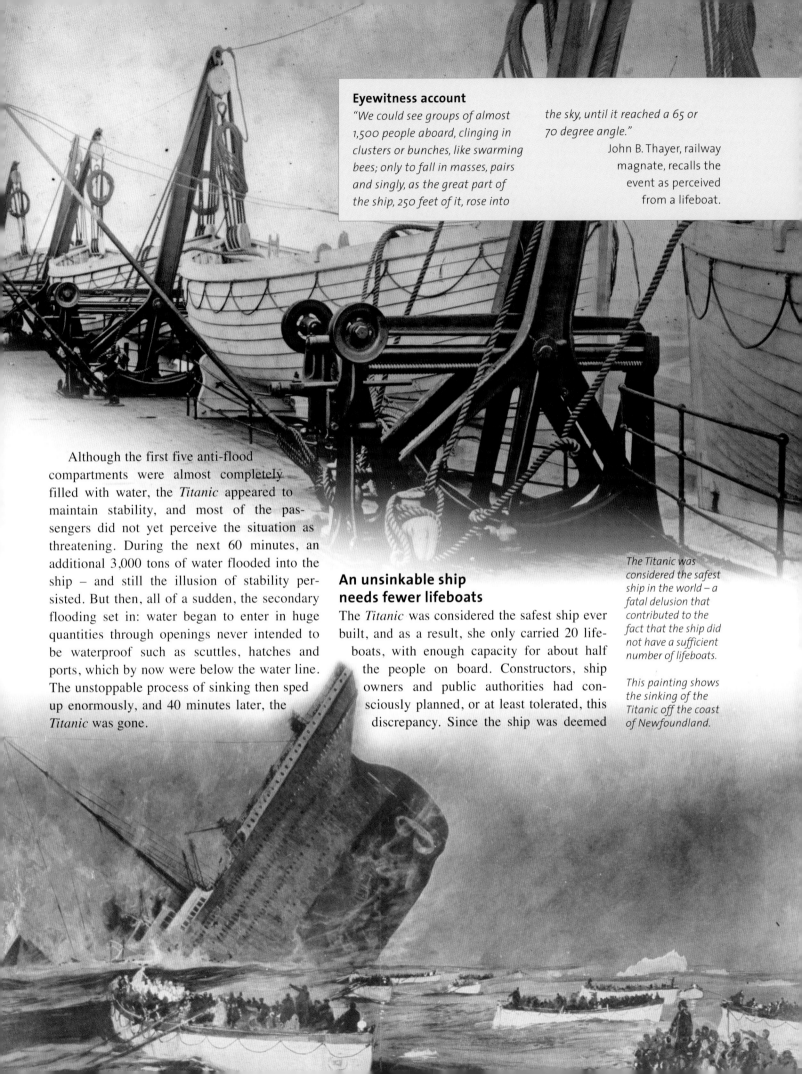

Although the first five anti-flood compartments were almost completely filled with water, the *Titanic* appeared to maintain stability, and most of the passengers did not yet perceive the situation as threatening. During the next 60 minutes, an additional 3,000 tons of water flooded into the ship – and still the illusion of stability persisted. But then, all of a sudden, the secondary flooding set in: water began to enter in huge quantities through openings never intended to be waterproof such as scuttles, hatches and ports, which by now were below the water line. The unstoppable process of sinking then sped up enormously, and 40 minutes later, the *Titanic* was gone.

An unsinkable ship needs fewer lifeboats

The *Titanic* was considered the safest ship ever built, and as a result, she only carried 20 lifeboats, with enough capacity for about half the people on board. Constructors, ship owners and public authorities had consciously planned, or at least tolerated, this discrepancy. Since the ship was deemed

The Titanic was considered the safest ship in the world – a fatal delusion that contributed to the fact that the ship did not have a sufficient number of lifeboats.

This painting shows the sinking of the Titanic off the coast of Newfoundland.

unsinkable, it did not need more lifeboats – or so the fatal line of reasoning. The lifeboats the *Titanic* did carry were mainly intended for saving survivors of other ships in distress. Moreover, lifeboats obviously required space, and that space was by preference used for the promenade deck, private decks and suites. The *Titanic* was originally intended to carry 64 lifeboats, but Bruce Ismay, chairman and director of the White Star Line, had campaigned for this number to be reduced by half in order to guarantee a better view from the promenade deck. Moreover, he argued, it was unwise to upset passengers who had paid for the luxury of travelling on an unsinkable ship by the sight of too many lifeboats. In the end, the number of lifeboats was reduced to 20.

The Carpathia receives Titanic's distress call and comes to the rescue

Shortly after midnight, Captain Edward J. Smith consulted with Thomas Andrews, one of the shipbuilders on board. After inspecting the damage, Andrews, exasperated with his failure, had no choice but to predict the quick and inevitable sinking of the ship. Smith then gave orders to send out distress calls around 0:15 a.m. Later that night, Captain Smith voluntarily stayed with his ship and drowned.

The *Carpathia* was the first to respond to *Titanic*'s distress signals and changed her course to come to the rescue, even though it took her four hours to reach the scene of the disaster. Meanwhile, most first class passengers refused to don life vests; since they could not perceive any tilt of the ship, they did not believe they were in an emergency situation. Sixty-five minutes after the collision, the first lifeboat was lowered. The idea of women and children first did not apply on the *Titanic* that fateful night. Rather, being rescued became a matter of what side of the ship passengers found themselves on and what class they had booked. Some port side officers determinedly imposed the "no men" principle, accepting that this resulted in half-full lifeboats being lowered when there were no more women willing to get on – people found it hard to believe that something so terrible was

A lifeboat is picked up by the Carpathia, which arrived at the scene of disaster two hours after Titanic's final distress call. By that time, the Titanic had already sunk.

actually happening. One survivor reported that it took great persuasion to get her 13-year-old son into a boat, as the officer on duty considered him a man. It was easier for men to get into a lifeboat on the starboard side, where many more lives were saved than on the port side. Tragically, although there was lifeboat capacity for 1,178 people, only 705 used them. While the tragedy unfolded, Wallace Hartley, conductor of the ship's orchestra, ordered the musicians to play entertaining music to help keep people calm. However, when both the passengers and crew realized that the unthinkable was actually happening, they were seized with panic. The ship had been flooded with some 40,000 tons of water, the decks were awash, the funnels were collapsing, and at about 2:18 a.m., the uneven weight of water burst the hull in two. The bow sank instantly. The stern reared upright in the air, and at 2:20 a.m. it sank, vertically, to a depth of 3,821 m (12,536 ft).

At 4:10 a.m., the *Carpathia* rescued a total of 705 survivors, but 1,522 people lost their lives in the catastrophe, dying in the ice-cold waters. Arthur Rostron, captain of the *Carpathia*, was left with the tragic duty of recovering the dead still floating in the sea.

Who was to blame?

Few of the victims actually died as the boat sank. Most died in the water, of hypothermia. Apart from lack of experience in the use of lifeboats in an emergency situation, subsequent analyses and investigations blamed the high death toll on an insufficient number of lifeboats. Ever since the *Titanic* sinking, all ships have been required to carry enough lifeboats to provide space for every passenger on board.

The commission set up to clarify the issue of liability ultimately held the following to blame for the tragedy: William M. Murdoch, First Officer of the *Titanic*; Joseph Bruce Ismay, Manager of the White Star Line; and Stanley Lord, Captain of the SS *Californian*, a ship that allegedly passed by the *Titanic* in immediate proximity without coming to its aid. Captain Lord, however, denied these accusations throughout his life.

The Titanic's grand dining hall. The ship was not only considered the safest in the world, but also the most splendid.

Auction sale of artifacts found in the Titanic wreck

On 10 June 2004, an auction was held at the South Street Seaport Museum in New York, in the vicinity of the Titanic memorial. Finds from the legendary wreck of the ocean liner were for sale.

Some interesting items among the hundreds for sale included:

• *Original menus: five items from the various restaurants and classes were up for sale*
• *White Star Line china*

• *Property from the luxury liner, including a lifeboat name plaque, a deck chair and a Titanic life jacket*
• *Rare photographs and autographs*
• *A collection of items relating to the life and death of John William Gill, one of the passengers*
• *Models of the ship*
• *Props from James Cameron's movie, Titanic*

Relieved and joyful friends and relatives of survivors of the Titanic catastrophe upon their arrival in Southampton.

FLU: THE UNDER-ESTIMATED THREAT

FROM SPANISH FLU TO AVIAN FLU

1918 was the final year of World War I, the war that had drawn in nearly all of Europe and claimed some 9 million lives all over the world. It was early in the year, and no one realized that the great catastrophe of the early twentieth century would not be this devastating war, after all, but a flu epidemic.

Bad news from Spain

The earliest reports of a massive flu epidemic came from Spain in the spring of 1918. Because Spain was not directly involved in World War I, the country censored news less strictly than others. The war-faring countries, by contrast, made every effort not to let terrifying news weaken their people's morale, which explains how this global epidemic came to be called the "Spanish" flu. Today, however, it is clearly understood that the illness did not originate in Spain.

The first cases probably occurred in March 1918 at an American military base in Kansas. The disease spreads rapidly, and within a very short period entire battalions were infected. Its contagiousness was badly underestimated, allowing the flu to spread rapidly among the soldiers' families, and it reached Europe with the arrival of the first American active service troops.

Waves of death

The Spanish flu spread in several waves. The first occurred in the spring of 1918 and abated in August of the same year. But the flu returned in the fall of 1918, originating this time from France. Again the disease was extremely contagious – but this time it was deadlier still. The epidemic mainly affected people between 18 and 35 years old (that is, people in their most productive years). The effects were so dramatic that public life was brought to a standstill in many places. Schools and other public institutions were forced to close, and face masks

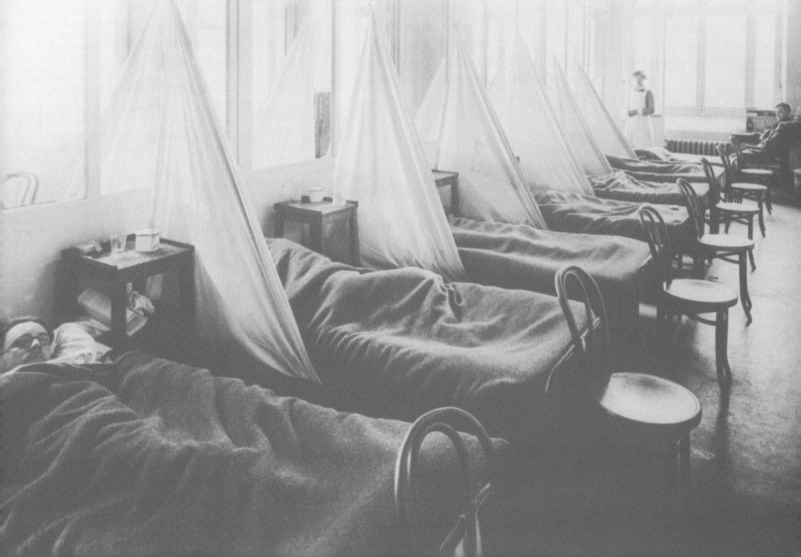

In the fall of 1918, the flu hit France. Huge numbers of US soldiers were treated in this military hospital.

When avian flu broke out in China, millions of poultry were destroyed.

were seen in every street. By early 1919, the worst was over. While there were further, smaller waves, most of the victims died during the first nine months of the crisis. When the flu finally receded in 1921, it had claimed 25 to 50 million lives worldwide, at least three times as many as World War I (which ended in 1918). The US Army lost more soldiers to the Spanish flu than died in combat.

A virus is the cause

Epidemics of such a catastrophic scale have come to be known as pandemics, a word derived from ancient Greek that literally means "concerning the entire population." Like epidemics, pandemics are also defined as occurring within a certain period of time. Unlike epidemics, however, pandemics are not limited to a particular geographic region; instead, they spread across all the continents. Pandemics comparable to the Spanish flu include the Black Death (1347–1352), which also claimed over 20 million lives, and AIDS, the immunodeficiency disease that has been rampant since the 1980s.

The powerlessness of medicine in the face of the widespread deaths caused by Spanish flu was partly due to the fact that the influenza virus was still unknown at that time. Scientists originally assumed that a bacterium caused the disease. There would have been no defence

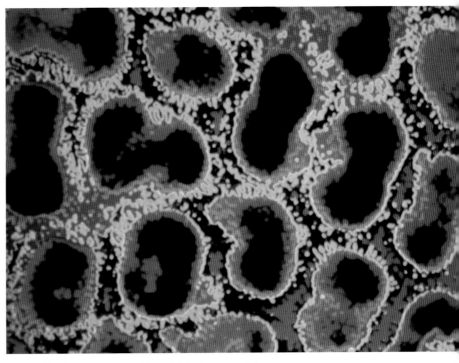

Originally, the disease was thought to be caused by a bacterium. The virus responsible for the flu was discovered in 1933.

against viruses anyway, since there were no methods available to detect them. It was not until 1933 that English researchers successfully isolated the influenza virus in animal experiments and, even then, the subtype that caused

the Spanish flu remained unknown. In 1951, scientists came closer to the cause by studying the bodies of victims of the influenza epidemic that had been conserved in the freeze-up of Alaska. This approach was not successful until 1997, when the American molecular biologist Jeffery Taubenberger finally solved the long-standing mystery. The 1918 killer virus had been of type A/H1N1, an extremely aggressive strain that uses birds as hosts before mutating to affect humans, as well.

The danger of mutations

The Spanish flu remained the most catastrophic virus epidemic of the modern age for some 40 years, as the world was spared further epidemics on a global scale. Then, in 1957 and 1958, another epidemic of global proportions occurred: the Asian flu. The disease originated in China and was carried to Hong Kong by refugees from Red China, and from there, it spread throughout the world. This pandemic

Types of influenza virus

The strains of human influenza virus can be divided into three types. Type B and C viruses affect humans almost exclusively and are relatively harmless. Type A, however, is both the most dangerous and the most widespread type of influenza virus. It not only affects humans, but also poultry and pigs. Type A occurs in various subtypes that are distinguished by names such as H1N1 or H5N1. Genetic transfers between avian flu viruses and human influenza

viruses give rise to deadly new subtypes for which humans have no antibodies (specialised cells to fight off the infection). The third big influenza epidemic to occur in the twentieth century, the Hong Kong flu of 1968, was also caused by mutations of a type A virus. In this case, a type-A H2N2 virus (which caused the Asian flu, below) recombined with an avian flu virus to form a new subtype, A/H3N2. This deadly mutation claimed approximately one million lives worldwide.

claimed 1 to 4 million lives within a relatively short period of time.

This particular flu virus descended from the A/H1N1 influenza virus (which had caused the Spanish flu) by recombination with an avian influenza virus. This produced a new virus – type A/H2N2 – against which the human immune system had no defence.

After this wave died down, many people had become immune to the virus and, as a result, the Asian flu has not circulated in decades. However, subsequent generations have developed very few antibodies against this particular strain of virus, and this could lead to catastrophic effects in the event of a new A/H2N2 epidemic.

In light of this historical background, the stir caused by a press release from the Robert Koch Institute in Berlin in April 2004 is understandable. The research institute stated that it had mistakenly sent samples of this virus to thousands of labs all over the world for routine testing. The World Health Organization immediately called on all of the labs to destroy the samples.

When will the next pandemic take place?

A new virus subtype that could cause the next big pandemic might develop at any moment through a recombination of human and animal influenza viruses. Asia seems especially prone to figure as the originating region of such mutations. The simple methods of animal husbandry practiced in Asia create favourable conditions for simultaneous infections of humans and animals. The H5N1 bird flu virus, which originated in Asia, has been rampant since 2003. Although it apparently has not combined with human influenza viruses yet, there is a real and ever-present danger that it will. It is estimated that a pandemic triggered by the H5N1 virus would claim between 7 and 150 million victims.

Following the outbreak of avian flu, there has been an ever-present fear of a new influenza epidemic in Asia. Hardly anyone dares to walk in the streets without wearing a face mask.

A famous victim: Egon Schiele

Famous victims of the flu include the Austrian painter Egon Schiele (1890–1918). This luminary of the Viennese art scene was 28 years old and had just been a pall-bearer for his patron and mentor Gustav Klimt (1862–1918), the most famous representative of Jugendstil, when he and his wife both became victims of the second wave of Spanish flu. At the time, Edith was six months pregnant. She died on 28 October 1918. Egon Schiele, who sketched his dying wife in agony, only survived her by three days.

Today, Schiele's works sell for record prices in international auctions.

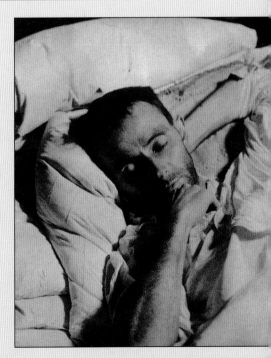

Egon Schiele on his deathbed.

Nuclear Holocaust

THE ATOMIC BOMBS OF HIROSHIMA AND NAGASAKI

In August 1945, World War II was over in Europe; in the Far East, however, it was still raging with no end in sight. American squadrons continued to execute air raids on Tokyo and other large cities. Hiroshima, the city on the delta of the Ota River, had thus far been spared the attacks. On the morning of 6 August 1945 that changed dramatically.

The Enola Gay drops its deadly payload

At 8:00 a.m. on that fateful day, a B-29 Super-fortress flew high above Hiroshima in the blazing sun. The Japanese assumed the plane was a reconnaissance aircraft – accustomed to attacks from squadrons, no one worried about a single aircraft. While people on the ground went about their daily business, the captain of the *Enola Gay*, Colonel Paul W. Tibbets, and his crew armed an atomic bomb for airdrop. This, the first weapon of mass destruction in human history, was euphemistically christened *Little Boy*. *Little Boy* was 3.3 m (11 ft) long and weighed over 4,000 kg (8,800 lbs).

The bomb was released over Hiroshima and fell to an altitude of 600 m (2,000 ft) before a nuclear fission and ensuing chain reaction was triggered that built up an explosive force equivalent to 20,000 tons of TNT. Hiroshima, a city of 390,000, was destroyed in a second, the ground completely flattened. It is estimated that at least 75,000 people were killed instantly, and up to 250,000 more fell victim to the fallout and long-term effects. Never in history has a single instrument of destruction anni-hilated so many lives and caused so much destruction as the bomb of 6 August 1945.

Metal melts

Any witnesses who survived this catastrophe were necessarily far from ground zero. Every-thing within a radius of 3 km (2 miles) was de-stroyed instantly; within 5 km (3 miles), a third of the houses were left standing but went up in flames shortly afterwards. Even very distant witnesses felt the bomb's shock wave before they saw the pillar of smoke rising some 18 km (11 miles) into the sky. Anything at the centre of the explosion was completely destroyed: the enormous temperature melted all metal, and everything else was consumed in the fire or blasted away. Any life in this centre was effec-tively pulverized. Around this, a tremendous wind fueled the fires. Only those who found themselves covered by debris or who were protected from the shock wave in any other way escaped immediate death.

Even those who survived, like everything else, were exposed to the penetrating gamma

A mushroom cloud hovered over the city of Hiroshima after the atomic bomb was dropped.

radiation emitted by the bomb (see box). Any living being within a 2.2-km (1.4-mile) radius experienced certain death, if not immediately, then shortly after the explosion. Everything was radioactively contaminated. There was no hope for the rescue teams that started arriving soon afterwards to do what they could in this most horrible situation: contact with all the contaminated matter meant death for them, too. It was impossible for anyone to take precautions or protect themselves: nobody, including the Americans, knew what terrifying consequences their actions would have.

Unspeakable suffering of the civilian population

For some of the victims, the nightmare came to a quick end; others continued to suffer un-

In August 1945, under the command of Colonel Paul W. Tibbets, the B-29 bomber plane Enola Gay dropped the first atomic bomb in history on the Japanese city of Hiroshima.

speakably from vomiting, diarrhoea, haemorrhages of the skin, lungs, bladder and stomach, recurring fever, hair loss and the breakdown of their stomach linings for weeks and even months. The victims had hardly any white blood cells left and died in agony. The people living in areas surrounding Hiroshima had a 50 per cent increased risk of contracting leukaemia in the years following the bombing.

The first weapon of mass destruction in history was named "Little Boy." Little Boy was 3.3 m (11 ft) long and weighed over 4,000 kg (8,800 lbs).

Gamma radiation

Some chemical elements have the property of emitting radiation without an external energy supply; this phenomenon is called radioactivity, and it depends on the instability of the atomic nucleus. Gamma rays, which are highly radioactive, form an extremely high-frequency type of radiation that occurs during nuclear decay and is highly penetrative. Gamma rays are weakened in proportion to the mass of the matter they pass through. An exploding atomic bomb emits a very high level of gamma radiation.

Gamma rays are also used for peaceful purposes, such as in cancer therapy and in tools and material testing.

The attack on Nagasaki

Even following this disastrous strike against its civilian population, Japan appeared to be unwilling to give in or surrender. Moreover, Russia declared war on Japan. The United States administration, under President Harry S. Truman, made a decision in favour of a second nuclear attack: on 8 August they dropped the plutonium bomb *Fat Man* on the industrial city of Nagasaki. *Fat Man* weighed 5,000 kg (11,000 lbs) and generated an infernal temperature of 300,000 °C (540,000 °F) that immediately annihilated any life. The shock wave, travelling at a speed of 14,000 km/87,000 miles per hour, wiped out the Nagasaki suburb below the bomb. More than 50,000 people died immediately. For the thousands who survived, again, there was no hope: as in the case of Hiroshima, they died painfully from the long-term effects of the explosion.

That finally brought the Pacific War to an end. On 15 August 1945 Emperor Hirohito announced Japan's surrender.

Hiroshima after the nuclear air attack on 6 August 1945: a scene of utter devastation. The one building that withstood the bombing, the Prefectural Industrial Promotion Hall, has been restored as a memorial.

Many other types of cancer, including lung, stomach, thyroid, ovarian and laryngeal cancer, occurred much more frequently, as well. Pregnant women experienced miscarriages or gave birth to horribly deformed babies who were barely able or unable to sustain life. To this day, more than 60 years after the attack, people in the region continue to suffer from the long-term health consequences.

Kiyoshi Kikkawa is one of countless burn victims of the Hiroshima atomic bombing. Two years after the bomb fell, he was still ravaged.

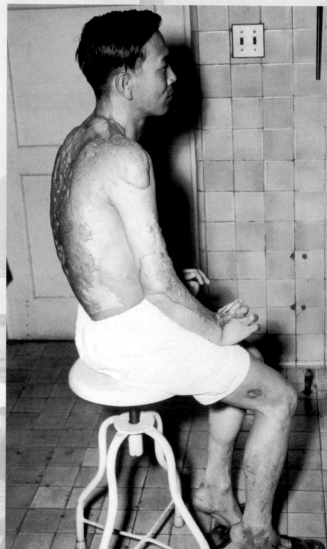

Julius Robert Oppenheimer

J. Robert Oppenheimer (1904–1967) is known as the father of the atomic bomb. From 1943, he was director of the Los Alamos research labs, where the first nuclear bombs were developed and produced. During the McCarthy Era, in 1954, he was dismissed from his position owing to former associations with communists, but was rehabilitated in 1963. Originally, Oppenheimer thought of his invention as the greatest in the history of mankind, but he later changed his mind. When he saw the extent of destruction caused by his "baby", he is said to have told president Harry S. Truman in despair: "I have blood on my hands." Truman allegedly replied that he never had any scruples about the affair. With regard to Japan, he is quoted as saying, "When you have to deal with a beast, you have to treat him as a beast."

Tests in the New Mexico desert

Just a few weeks earlier, on 16 July 1945, the Americans had detonated an atomic bomb for the first time in a test area in the state of New Mexico. Dr. J. Robert Oppenheimer (1904–1967; see box opposite), leader of the scientific team that developed these weapons, spoke of the "birth of a very special baby" – hence the diminutive, euphemistic name for the Hiroshima bomb, *Little Boy*. When he and his fellow scientists at the Los Alamos labs (where atomic bombs were built from 1943, and where research in the maintenance of existing nuclear arms continues today) saw the enormous effects and the destructive potential of their "baby", they experienced a rush of megalomania. They had no way of knowing the long-term damage and effects of the bomb. Edward Teller, one of the physicists working at Los Alamos, told people, "If your mountain is not in the right place, drop us a postcard." Three weeks later, the first atomic bombs were dropped on people.

The balance of terror

In the more than 60 years that have passed since the dropping of these two bombs – fortunately, further atomic bombs have not been used against humans in meantime – a situation emerged in the aftermath of World War II and against the backdrop of the Cold War immediately following it, that became known as the "Balance of Terror". When the Russians developed the capacity to build nuclear weapons themselves, an arms race ensued that was unlike anything the world had ever seen. Nuclear superpowers armed themselves with so many weapons that they could have blown up the world several times over if, on any given day, anything had gone wrong enough to cause one of the world leaders to press the notorious "red button". For a while it seemed that that risk had come under control: the parties approached each other and declared the arms race officially over. Today, however, the danger of nuclear destruction also comes from other nations and institutions, and not only from the former Soviet Union and the USA.

Japanese schoolgirls wearing face masks to help them endure the stench of decay and contamination.

Harry S. Truman

Harry S. Truman (1984–1972), the 33rd president of the USA, served two terms in office from 1945 until 1953. After the end of World War II he increased pressure on the Soviet Union after 1947, which culminated in the founding of NATO in 1949. Truman was known as a political hardliner who extended the Cold War and who stood by his view that the use of the atomic bombs had been necessary. Together with Senator Joseph McCarthy, he got the US embroiled in a witch hunt for communists, who were supposedly undermining the country. Even after his terms as president, he wrote a letter to the Hiroshima City Council in which he stated that given the same circumstances, he would again order a nuclear strike.

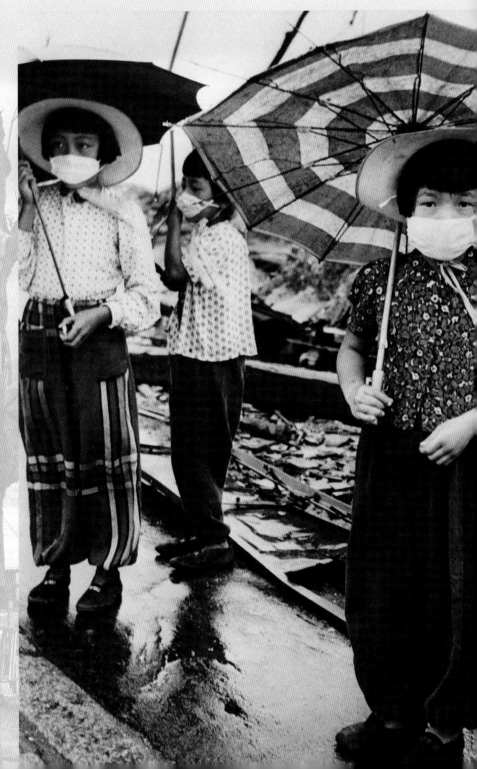

1967

Oil on the Coasts of Europe

THE TANKERS *TORREY CANYON* AND *AMOCO CADIZ* POLLUTE THE ATLANTIC COAST

In March 1967, the first massive oil disaster in the history of tanker shipping struck a European coast. The *Torrey Canyon* hit a reef, causing an environmental catastrophe of unprecedented proportions. While maritime safety measures were increased on a global scale in the aftermath of this disaster, supertankers remain a threat to the environment. Eleven years later, human failure led to the next enormous oil spill: the *Amoco Cadiz* sank off the coast of Brittany, badly polluting that coastline.

The Torrey Canyon accident

In 1967, a new kind of catastrophe reached the coasts of Europe. For some time, the industrial nations' rapidly growing demand for crude oil had made it necessary to build oil tankers of ever increasing size. The supertanker *Torrey Canyon* herself, built in 1959 with a capacity of 60,000 tons, had been adapted at a later time to enable her to carry double her original cargo of crude oil, making the ship correspondingly cumbersome to navigate. Moreover, this enlargement made her a member of a class of ships which, according to international agreements, was only authorized to travel along certain routes that were considered particularly safe. Unfortunately, on 18 March 1967, the *Torrey Canyon* left the safe route owing to a navigational error, and then struck the notorious Seven Stones Reef off the coast of Land's End, the westernmost point of the English coastline. The ship sprang a leak and spilled 120,000 tons of oil into the Atlantic Ocean. For the first time in history, an oil spill polluted European shores.

The woefully inept response to the catastrophe

Even as the accident was taking place, the disastrous lack of experience in responding to this kind of environmental disaster became appallingly clear as a series of attempts to control the damage actually resulted in compounding the problems. In the first instance, efforts were directed towards making the ship functional again. After several days of this unsuccessful endeavour, the ship broke apart while it was still impaled on the reef. Meanwhile, the oil layer on the sea continued to grow and grow, and also threatened coasts on both sides of the Channel: the Cornish coast in England and the Normandy coast in France. An effort was therefore made to burn off the oil spill – but this did not have the intended effect, either. Finally, the British Army bombed the wreckage. In an attempt to break up the oil slick, extensive use of detergents was made – but this turned out to be even more detrimental to marine life than the oil itself.

About a week after the accident, the Torrey Canyon broke into two halves, still stranded on the Seven Stones reef off the coast of Cornwall.

The bow of the stricken supertanker Amoco Cadiz, projecting from the water like the mouth of a gigantic whale.

The Suez Canal and supertankers

The Suez Canal is a link between the Indian Ocean and the Mediterranean Sea. After World War II, it became the ideal route for transporting crude oil from oil producing regions on the Arab Peninsula to the industrial consumers in Europe in a quick and inexpensive manner. However, the dimensions of the canal made it necessary to introduce a size limit for ships.

From 5 to 10 June 1967, during the Six Day War between Israel and its Arab neighbours Egypt, Syria and Jordan, the Suez Canal became the front line between Israel and Egypt. Ships that sank in the canal in during the clashes made it impassable, and eight years passed before the wrecks were salvaged, thus clearing the passage so that it could be reopened for international shipping.

Around this time ocean carriers started building supertankers because oil from the Arab countries now had to be shipped to Europe by the circuitous southern route around the African continent. Using this route, which was much longer, profitability could only be achieved by employing very large tankers, and this was attractive since the size limitations for the Suez Canal no longer applied. The world's largest tanker in 1955, the Al Malik Saud Al Awal, could carry 47,000 tons of crude oil. The world's largest ship 50 years later, the tanker Jahre Viking, had a capacity over ten times higher: 564,673 tons.

Consequences of the first oil spill

The situation after these misguided efforts was shocking: 190 km (120 miles) of the English coast and 80 km/50 miles of the French coast were badly contaminated. More than 15,000 sea birds died an agonizing death, and countless marine organisms were destroyed. Europe, however, had been stirred: from then on, the general public took greater interest in environmental health issues. Legal provisions for the operation and traffic of tankers was tightened significantly and eventually, in 1973, an international agreement was passed. MARPOL73, the International Convention for the Prevention of Marine Pollution from Ships, is internationally recognized and is still in force today.

The next apocalypse

In spite of tightened international regulations, supertankers remain environmental time bombs; their impact depends not only on technology, but also on human action in emergencies. In the early hours of 16 March 1978, 24 km (15 miles) off the Breton coast, the rudder unit of the tanker *Amoco Cadiz* failed. The tanker, which carried 223,000 tons of crude oil, drifted helplessly. In the teeth of strong west winds pushing

Despite the bombing of the ship by the Royal Navy, part of the Torrey Canyon *still had not sunk on 30 March 1967.*

the tanker towards the coast, the crew initially tried to repair the rudder unit themselves. Almost two hours after the failure, the captain finally requested a tugboat to help move the ship's bow into the wind so it could steer away from the coast independently. Unfortunately, the requested tug was not powerful enough to bring the supertanker into the right position, and a stronger boat arrived on the scene too late. At 9:00 p.m., the *Amoco Cadiz* ran into a rock off

Two weeks after the Amoco Cadiz broke apart, the Breton coast was completely polluted by oil. Volunteer helpers fought a desperate battle.

the French coast. While the crew could be successfully rescued by helicopter, the tanker broke apart the same night. A 360-km (225-mile) stretch of the Breton coast was contaminated by crude oil. About 28 million sea animals – fish, conches and more – died in a single day.

Spilled oil coats and congeals the feathers of sea birds, which is why these creatures die in enormous numbers in the aftermath of an oil spill.

Major Oil Spills

YEAR	SHIP	COAST	OIL SPILLED
1967	Torrey Canyon	Cornwall (England)	120,000 t
1976	Urquillo	North Spain	100,000 t
1978	Amoco Cadiz	Brittany (France)	230,000 t
1978	Andros Patria	North Spain	50,000 t
1992	Aegean Sea	North Spain	70,000 t
1996	Sea Empress	Wales (England)	147,000 t
1999	Erika	Brittany (France)	20,000 t
2002	Prestige	Spain	77,000 t

AVOID INFECTION AT ALL COSTS

THE AIDS PANDEMIC

"In America you see people living with HIV, like Magic Johnson. In Africa people die of AIDS; it's a death sentence", said two-time Grammy nominated singer India Arie in an interview with Nekesa Mumbi Moody after her visit to Kenya. "It's a very rare person who gets antiviral drugs. Try to understand what that really looks like: a 70-year-old woman doing manual labour to take care of 6-, 7- and 8-year-olds because the whole genera-tion, the middle generation, has been wiped out. I saw that over and over again."

These children and teenagers in Lagos, Nigeria are pro-testing child abuse and the threat of an AIDS infection from a paedophile living in their neighbourhood.

Acquired Immune Deficiency Syndrome

In 2005 alone, more than 3 million people died of this disease and some 5 million became newly infected. AIDS – Acquired Immune De-ficiency Syndrome – is truly a global epidemic. It began to emerge about 25 years ago and has already claimed more than 25 million lives.

Currently, some 40 million people are living with HIV, the virus that eventually leads to AIDS, among them an ever-growing number of women and children.

Epicentre: Africa

The AIDS epicentre is Africa. According to the organization UNAIDS, only 10 per cent of the world's population lives in this region, yet it has 60 per cent of all AIDS patients. The following figures provide an overview of the current distribution of AIDS:
– Africa: 25.8 million
– Asia: 8.3 million
– Latin America: 1.8 million
– Eastern Europe and Central Asia: 1.6 million
– North America: 1.2 million
– Western and Central Europe: 720,000
– North Africa/Middle East: 510,000
– Caribbean: 300,000
– Oceania: 74,000
In Eastern Europe and Asia in particular, the number of infected persons has been rising disproportionately rapidly in recent years.

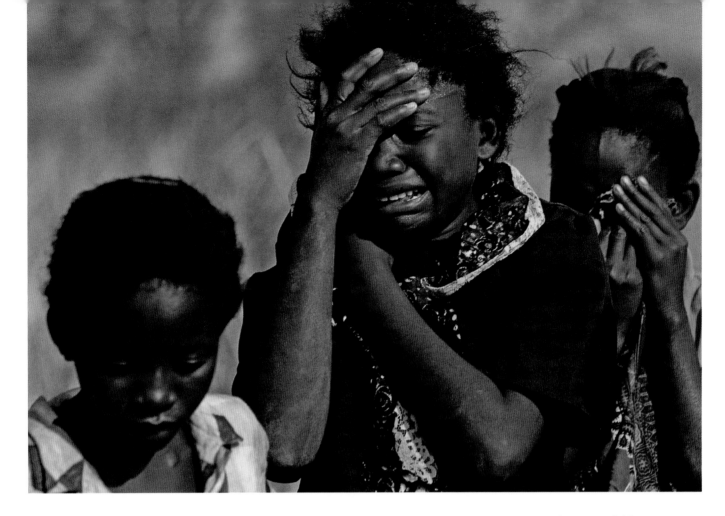

What is the difference between HIV and AIDS? The first causes the latter. "HI" stands for "human immunodeficiency". HI viruses destroy human antibodies, thereby weakening the immune system. This prevents the immune system doing its job, which is to fight intrusive fungi, bacteria or viruses. An HIV-infected person will become sicker than they should when they contract an illness that their body in a healthy state would be able to fend off easily. AIDS, therefore, is the late stage of an HIV infection.

AIDS viruses have a particularly long incubation period (that is, a long time may go by between infection and when the first symptoms start to show). During that time, before they even know they carry the virus, HIV-infected people can pass the disease to others.

Children mourning their mother. Given the lack of homes and schools in Africa, most AIDS orphans are entirely on their own.

How does HIV work?

Whenever pathogens enter the body, helper cells (also known as CD4 cells, T4 cells or T4 helper cells) fight them off. Helper cells are a specialized kind of white blood cells (leukocytes). HI viruses attack precisely these helper cells before they start spreading. The human body tries to counter-attack the viruses with antibodies, but fails. The viruses proliferate, and this is frequently followed by an immunological overreaction. The immune system is working flat out and may start attacking the body's own cells (autoimmune diseases). Patients are also more likely to suffer from allergies.

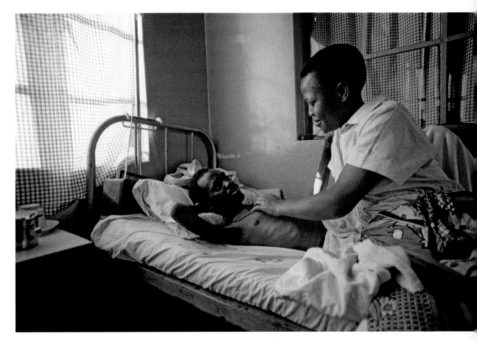

A woman tends her husband, who is suffering from AIDS, in a hospital in Rubwe (Tanzania).

35

At least 20 per cent
of the adult popu-
lation of Ndola,
Zambia suffers
from AIDS. The
cemeteries are
overcrowded.

How is AIDS transmitted?

Contrary to popular belief, HI viruses cannot
be transmitted by mosquito bites, coughs or
sneezes. About 80 per cent of all infections are
caused by vaginal, anal or oral sexual inter-
course with an infected partner and without
protection. The virus is found in semen and in
vaginal secretions. From there, it can enter the
body through the mucous membranes or
through small scratches in the skin. Immediately after infection, the patient is a particularly
high infection risk to others because the
number of viruses in their body is especially
high at this point. People already suffering
from an STD are particularly vulnerable.

The fact that viruses can be transmitted via
blood transfusions was realized relatively late.
In fact, the risk of infection is particularly high
in this case. Since 1985, blood donors in many
countries have been tested for AIDS, but these
tests are often not performed in developing
countries due to their cost. Drug addicts shar-
ing needles or syringes are at very high risk.
About 15 per cent of the AIDS patients in the
USA and Europe have been infected this way.

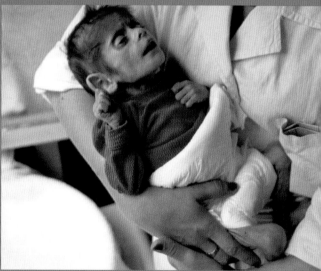

In the 1980s and 1990s, Romania saw a big increase
in children contracting AIDS. This baby in a Bucharest
hospital is ravaged by the disease.

People working in the medical field can contract infections when handling syringes or
insufficiently sterilized surgical instruments;
fortunately, however, such infections are rare.
Organ transplants are another potential source

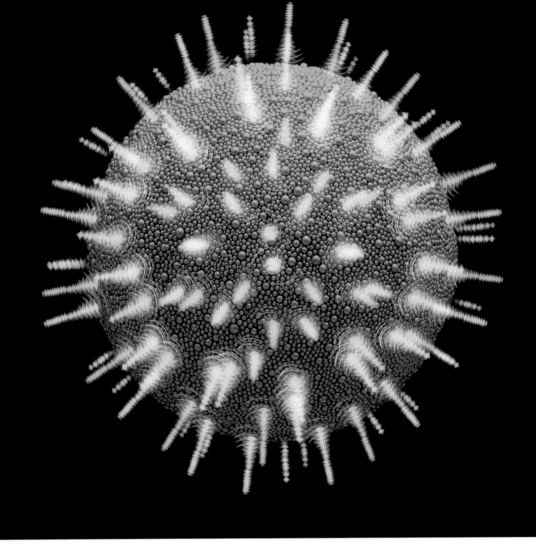

of infection, and infected mothers may pass the virus to their unborn babies. If treatment is begun during pregnancy, however, the risk of infection can be lowered by about two-thirds; C-section birth can reduce the risk further.

First test, then get treatment

Tests can determine whether an HI infection is present. At least 12 weeks after infection, these tests deliver very sound results. An HIV antibody test determines whether a person's body has taken measures against the intruder (i.e., whether it has developed antibodies against the HIV proteins). Further tests can identify antibodies against the virus, as well as the virus itself. "HIV-positive" means that antibodies are present and, by inference, that the virus has entered the body and has to be fought. The course of the disease varies widely, ranging from an almost complete lack of symptoms to fully developed AIDS syndrome including fever, diarrhoea, pneumonia, toxoplasmosis, herpes, Kaposi's sarcoma (a type of skin cancer), changes in the blood count, tuberculosis,

carcinomas, etc. The number of helper cells per microlitre of blood indicates the severity of the disease (500–1200 = normal, less than 250 = problematic). Whether and how soon these symptoms manifest varies greatly depending on a patient's overall health, their living conditions, the time elapsed since infection and the kind of medical treatment received. In the industrial countries, there are AIDS patients who have been living with the disease for as long as 15 years without suffering many symptoms.

A greatly enlarged HI virus. It was first identified by scientists in Paris in 1983.

Combined therapy helps

In the past, an AIDS diagnosis amounted to a death sentence. Now, however, there are improved therapies and combination drugs that enable many patients to experience a long symptom-free phase. The situation in developing countries is entirely different: the high prices of the drugs make it impossible to take them regularly.

This has led to great criticism and protests of pharmaceutical companies and their price policies. A critical problem consists in super-infections (that is, when an AIDS patient is re-infected with a second AIDS virus from a different virus group). This tends to occur among people who have a large number of sexual partners, such as prostitutes.

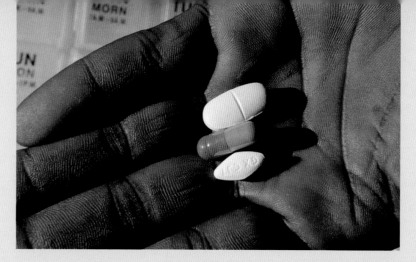

A South African AIDS patient's medication. Many people in Africa cannot afford the medication; they are treated irregularly, if at all.

Advertising for condoms in Abidjan on the Côte d'Ivoire. Used correctly and consistently, condoms considerably reduce the risk of an AIDS infection.

A complicated story

It is not known exactly when AIDS developed. It probably originated in Africa, when the virus jumped from chimpanzees to people. The earliest cases occurred in the late 1970s, and by 1980 it was present on a global scale. In 1981, an aggressive form of Kaposi's sarcoma was diagnosed in a young homosexual man in New York. Two cases of exceptionally rare types of pneumonia were diagnosed in New York and in California the same year. The occurrence of such unusual diseases attracted doctors' attention. At first the symptoms seem to be restricted to homosexuals, but soon drug addicts and haemophiliacs were among those infected with the disease, which was named AIDS in 1982 (SIDA in French and Spanish).

In 1983, researchers at the Parisian Pasteur Institute identified the virus. This led to panic: police officers started wearing masks and gloves when arresting potentially infected suspects, and social workers refused to meet with their clients and talked to them by phone instead. AIDS patients seemed to contract their infection mostly in contact with Americans or Africans, many of them from Zambia or Zaire, and especially in homosexual circles. In 1983, WHO listed 3,064 cases in the USA, 40 per cent of whom had died. In 1984, the American doctor Robert Gallo isolated the virus (called HTLV-III) and announced a test for determining its presence, which came on the market soon after.

Fear and discrimination

AIDS patients and representatives of the gay emancipation movement struggled against discrimination. Some parents, for instance, would not let their children go to school with young AIDS patients. The first famous person to die from AIDS was actor and ladies' man Rock Hudson, who died on 3 October 1985. The fear of AIDS continued to grow in spite of public campaigns supported by the likes of Princess Diana, who shocked the public in 1987 when she shook an AIDS patient's hand without pro-

tective gloves. In San Francisco, the gay community created a giant quilt made from patches bearing victims' names, and groups such as ACT UP or Gran Fury work towards improving knowledge about and treatment of AIDS all over America. AIDS patients are no longer allowed to enter the USA, and doctors have discussed whether medical secrecy applies if there is a risk of an infected person communicating the disease to a sexual partner. As late as 1998, an AIDS activist was beaten to death in South Africa by her neighbours when she publicly announced that she had been infected.

Setbacks and progress

In 1990, many people in France were infected through contaminated blood transfusions, even though tests had been theoretically available for a long time. Some of those responsible were later sentenced to prison terms, including Michel Garretta, former director of the French National Blood Transfusion Centre. In 1998, even the French prime minister, Laurent Fabius, had to appear before the court. In Romania, almost 100,000 orphans have been infected by blood transfusions. In Asia and Eastern Europe, the disease spreads implacably. Ever since 1994, anyone travelling to Russia has to undergo an AIDS test. By 1995, AIDS had become the most significant cause of death in the USA among the 25–44 age group. In its struggle against AIDS, the UN established UNAIDS, a joint program of WHO, the UNDP, UNICEF, the UNFPA, UNESCO and the World Bank.

The search for a vaccine, financially supported by former US president Bill Clinton and the Bill and Melinda Gates Foundation, turns out to be more complicated than expected. Condoms, special microbicide-based "condoms" for women, diaphragms and circumcision for men provide varying levels of protection against AIDS, as do education and abstinence.

The giant San Francisco quilt, shown here during an exhibition in commemoration of AIDS victims in Washington D.C., makes a lasting impression on visitors.

Robert Mapplethorpe: defeated by AIDS

New York photographer Robert Mapplethorpe, born in 1946, made photographic portraits of his friend Patti Smith (the cover of her first album, Horses, *features a photo by Mapplethorpe), as well as Richard Gere, Peter Gabriel, Grace Jones and Andy Warhol. He won his greatest fame, though, with controversial black-and-white photos portraying the gay community. These images triggered a heated debate about pornography in America. Mapplethorpe allegedly maintained sexual relations with 75 per cent of his male models, and he was known for his excessive drug consumption. After he contracted AIDS in 1986, he fought the disease with all his might. He was shocked to see so many of his friends die of GRID (Gay Related Immune Deficiency) –*

the term AIDS was not common back then. In his devastating 1988 self-portrait, he has the mark of death already on him. With medical treatment not resulting in the hoped-for effects, he was confined to a wheelchair by that time. Moreover, he was mourning his partner, the art collector Sam Wagstaff. In May 1988, ten months before his death, he decided to establish a foundation with the proceeds of a sale of his works. Apart from promoting photography, the purpose of this foundation is the fight against AIDS, with a focus on nursing long-term patients. Robert Mapplethorpe died of AIDS at the age of 42 on 9 March 1989. Patricia Morrisroe has recounted his life in a biography entitled This Charming Man.

1974

SWATHES OF DESTRUCTION

THE SUPER OUTBREAK: 148 TORNADOES RAMPAGE THROUGH AMERICA

In April 1974, no fewer than 148 tornados raged across the United States within 18 hours. This disaster, known as the Super Outbreak, left over 300 people dead and caused damage totaling $3,500,000,000. Thirteen states were afflicted by this – the biggest series of tornadoes there has ever been – suffering serious damage. According to recent research, such an intense series of tornadoes can be expected to occur only once every 500 years.

It began in Illinois

The weather forecast for North America on Wednesday 3 April 1974 anticipated some rain showers on the East Coast and thunderstorms in the Midwest. Children went to school, adults went to work, life carried on as usual. Then, around lunchtime, the first tornado developed over Morris, a small town in Illinois – a relatively harmless whirlwind that was more of a local land spout than a genuine tornado. Further eastward, it had been sunny all day, but then a storm front moving in an easterly direction arrived and the accompanying tornadoes grew in intensity. By the time the tornadoes reached the eastern border of the state of Illinois, they had already accounted for the first two deaths, and individual twisters were attaining category F3, which means they were strong enough to overturn vehicles.

A threatening tornado approaches. An apparently peaceful country idyll can be totally devastated in mere minutes.

The tornadoes reach Indiana

Monticello, Indiana experienced the first F4 tornado, which rampaged over almost 200 km (120 miles) before it dispersed. In the process, it created the longest swathe of destruction caused by any tornado during the Super Out-break. This tornado alone left 19 people dead and more than 300 seriously injured. Within

An F4 tornado is capable of shifting wooden houses with weak foundations or even overturning them, as shown in this photo from Texas.

minutes, the small town of Monticello was transformed into a scene of unimagineable destruction. Even sturdy official buildings such as the courthouse, the local high school and a Presbyterian church suffered serious damage. The headquarters of the local TV channel was simply blown away, almost without a trace.

The ordeal of the small town of Xenia, Ohio

The storm front, in which new tornadoes were continually forming, moved eastwards and reached the bordering state of Ohio just before 5 p.m. The 37th tornado of the day developed into a tornado of category F5, the highest category of tornado that has ever been measured on earth to date. With wind speeds of more than 400 km/290 miles per hour, such a tornado rips apart anything that lies in its path: even road surfaces are literally sucked from the ground. It struck the small town of Xenia, Ohio, which lies in an area that was already known to the Native Americans as the "place of deadly winds". Indeed, local records report more than 20 tornadoes in the area since 1884 alone. The 1974 tornado left 34 dead, 1,150 people injured and an additional 10,000 homeless. With nine schools, nine churches and approximately 180 businesses destroyed, half of the town lay in ruins.

A tornado of category F5 on the Fujita scale is capable of literally sucking away large chunks of tarred road.

One Super Outbreak tornado hit the town of Xenia, Ohio. One wall of this house was blown away, yet the furniture remained almost undamaged inside it – the pictures are still hanging on the walls.

13 states declared disaster areas

For 18 hours the storm front continued its progress, continually forming local tornadoes in the process. After the fact, a total of 148 tornadoes were registered, six of them reaching the feared level of category F5. In the end, the entire American Midwest was hit by this series, as well as New York state in the east and Alabama and Georgia to the south. To the north, the effects were felt as far away as the Canadian province of Ontario. The terror finally ended at 7 a.m. the following morning. The Super Outbreak had claimed between 315 and 330 lives, left inconceivable damage, and would enter the history books as the biggest tornado series in American history.

The Fujita scale

The storm researcher Tetsuya Fujita (1920–1998) developed a scale for categorizing tornadoes according to their wind speeds and destructive potential. The scale comprises 13 categories, *from F0 to F12, of which only the first five levels have been observed to date. From F6 upwards, the categories are thus theoretical.*

Categ.	Maximum wind speed	Damage
F0	115 km/75 miles per hour	Shallow-rooted trees and billboards overturned
F1	180 km/110 miles per hour	Tiles peeled off roofs, moving vehicles blown off roads
F2	250 km/155 miles per hour	Roofs torn off, large trees uprooted, light objects become dangerous missiles
F3	330 km/205 miles per hour	Trains derailed, cars overturned, woods uprooted
F4	420 km/260 miles per hour	Wooden houses with weak foundations blown some distance, trucks overturned
F5	515 km/320 miles per hour	Wooden houses destroyed, tarred roads partially sucked from the ground

An American military aircraft sprays the herbicide Agent Orange over a forest during the Vietnam War. The goal of the defoliation campaign was to prevent the enemy from disappearing into the jungle.

1976

AGENT ORANGE AND THE SEVESO DIOXIN CLOUD

THE EXTREMELY TOXIC COMPOUND KNOWN AS DIOXIN HAS THREATENED MANKIND FOR THE PAST HALF CENTURY.

Dioxin is one of the most toxic substances ever created. Over the past 50 years, its effect on people and the environment has been catastrophic. During the Vietnam War, it served as a key component in the chemical defoliation compound known as Agent Orange. In 1976 in the Italian city of Seveso, dioxin was released in a toxic aerosol cloud after an accident at a chemical factory. More recently, the deliberate dioxin poisoning of an Ukrainian presidential candidate led to public uproar and widespread unrest.

Operation Ranch Hand

In the 1960s, American troops were embroiled in the longstanding conflict between communist North Vietnam and the more Western-oriented South Vietnam. The Vietnam War was fought for the most part in terrain that was as much as three-quarters covered with dense jungle. The heavy vegetation, and the cover it provided for North Vietnamese guerrillas, was the American army's most pressing problem. Operation "Ranch Hand" was devised to drive the enemy out from under the forest canopy through defoliation of those dense forests. From 1962 to 1971, aeroplanes and helicopters dropped or sprayed herbicides over large areas. The most effective defoliation mixture was the one that went by the now infamous code name "Agent Orange". Agent Orange was a cocktail of chemicals that included a small amount of

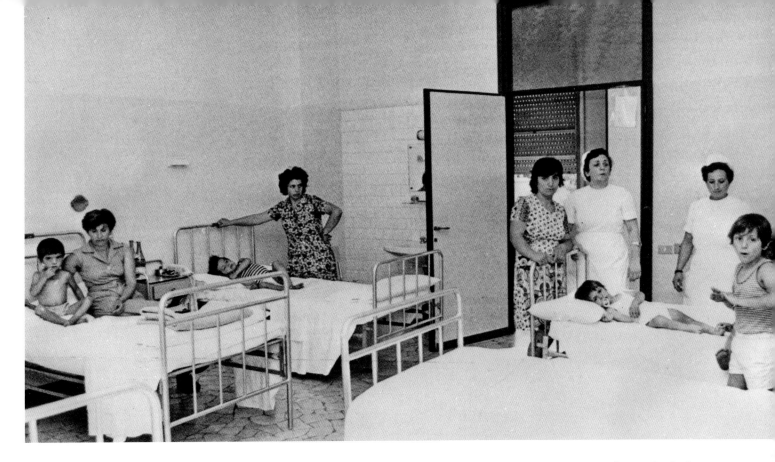

dioxin. Over the years, given the sheer quantity of Agent Orange used, the amount of dioxin released into the environment came to several hundred pounds. Due to the exceptional stability of dioxin, which breaks down only very slowly, the long-term effects of Agent Orange were catastrophic. Even today, decades after the end of the war, around 100,000 Vietnamese suffer from dioxin-related medical conditions, or from genetic diseases related to their parents' or even their grandparents' exposure. Dioxin attacks human DNA, leading to many generations of serious birth defects. American soldiers exposed to Agent Orange were also affected.

The poison cloud of Seveso

Dioxin was also involved in one of the worst environmental catastrophes of the 20th century. At 12:37 p.m. on 10 July 1976, human error caused a mixing vat in a small chemical factory near Seveso, Italy to explode. The factory (ICMESA, or Industri Chimiche Meda Società Azionaria), which usually made cosmetics, was enveloped in a cloud of poison gas that drifted slowly over the town of Seveso and several surrounding villages. For a full week, the factory tried to keep the accident secret. Finally, they began to evacuate the region. The cloud carried 2 kg (4.5 lbs) of highly toxic dioxin, enough to make the region around Seveso uninhabitable

Following the dioxin accident near Seveso, contaminated children filled local hospitals.

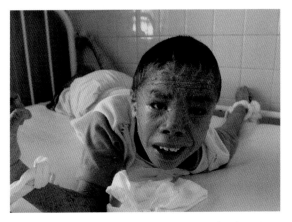

Vietnam is still struggling to overcome the long-term effects of dioxin poisoning. Birth defects caused by genetic damage have continued into the third generation.

Super-poison dioxin
After World War II, the German professor Wilhelm Sandermann (1906–1994) conducted research into the chemistry of wood and related organic compounds. He first described the compound TCDD (tetrachlordibenzo-p-dioxin) in a 1957 paper. Dioxin is a by-product of the chemical reaction that produces resins used to protect wood. Of all the known dioxin compounds, TCDD is by far the most toxic. Ingesting as little as one microgram per kg/2 lb body weight can be deadly. The poison attacks the cells and their DNA and causes severe liver damage and a disfiguring skin condition called chloracne. A connection between dioxin and cancer has long been suspected, though research is inconclusive. Dioxin breaks down very slowly, leading to long-term effects on the environment. Areas affected by dioxin contamination remain toxic for many years.

for many years. Hundreds of people suffered severe skin damage, and 75,000 poisoned animals had to be slaughtered. Long-term effects comparable to the dioxin-related conditions observed after the Vietnam War have not yet been studied for the Seveso disaster.

A policeman wearing protective clothing and a gas mask sets up signs around the town of Seveso warning people away from the area affected by the poisonous cloud.

The missing barrels of poison

Decontamination of the area affected by the Seveso dioxin cloud began in October 1976. It took until 1982 for all the affected materials, including the poisoned earth itself, to be removed. Initially, no attempt was made to clean up the area immediately around the exploded vat. In the summer of 1982, volunteer workers wearing heavy protective clothing took on this highly dangerous task. The debris was packed in barrels and transported north towards France. Shortly thereafter, the press discovered that the barrels had disappeared, and a far-reaching scandal ensued. Officials searched for the barrels for months, eventually finding them in May 1983 in northern France. In 1985, following the introduction of new incineration technology that leaves little or no residue, the barrels of poison were finally burned in Basel, Switzerland.

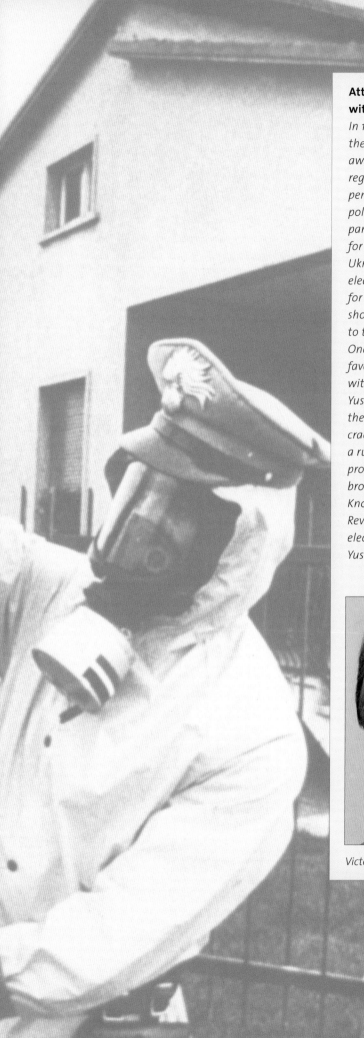

Attempted assassination with dioxin

In 1991, as the states constituting the Soviet Union began to break away, the Ukraine, like the others, regained its status as an independent nation. Nevertheless, political relations with its former partner states remained in place for many years. In 2004, the Ukranian national presidential election developed into a forum for deciding whether the Ukraine should orient itself to the west or to the east.

One candidate, Viktor Yanukovitch, favoured a closer relationship with Russia. His opponent, Viktor Yushchenko, wanted to open up the country to Western democracies. When Yanukovitch won a run-off election, non-violent protests demanding a recount broke out all across the Ukraine. Known to history as the Orange Revolution, the protests led to new elections that were won by Yushchenko.

The election itself, however, was overshadowed by suspicions that Yushchenko was the victim of an assassination attempt involving deliberate poisoning with dioxin. Following a dinner with the head of the Ukrainian secret service, Yushchenko fell ill with symptoms of severe poisoning. He was so debilitated that continuing the campaign proved to be impossible. The effects on his health were especially visible in his face. Within the span of just a few weeks, a vital, handsome politician aged dramatically, owing to the progress of what looks like dioxin-related chloracne. Suspicions regarding deliberate poisoning were confirmed in December 2004 following a series of medical tests in a Vienna hospital. A blood sample taken from Yushchenko showed a dioxin concentration 1,000 times the normal level. Later investigation by the medical board of the Ukraine confirmed the diagnosis.

Victor Yushchenko before and after being poisoned with dioxin.

1980

A MOUNTAIN EXPLODES

THE ERUPTION OF MOUNT ST. HELENS

Because of its symmetrical beauty, Mount St. Helens in the north west American state of Washington is also known as the Mount Fuji of America. Eternal ice and snow shimmer idyllically on its peak – or did so until 18 May 1980, when the volcano erupted – completely unpredicted – after an earthquake triggered a landslide of the entire northern flank. The release of pent-up pressure caused the numerous explosions that followed and an avalanche of rocks, boulders, ash and ice destroyed everything in its path for hundreds of miles. More than 60 people lost their lives in this natural catastrophe.

Ash was catapulted 19 km (11 miles) into the stratosphere. The columns of smoke could be seen from a great distance.

Naming the mountain

Between 1792 and 1794, Commander George Vancouver and his crew aboard the expedition ship HMS *Discovery* explored the Pacific coast of North America. Early on in this journey, in October of 1792, they gave the towering volcano on the west coast of America the name Mount St. Helens – after the British diplomat Alleyne Fitzherbert (1753–1839), who bore the title of Baron St. Helens.

Mount St. Helens is surrounded by several "brother" peaks. Mount Adams is about 50 km

(30 miles) distant; roughly 80 km (48 miles) away is the gigantic cascade volcano of Mount Rainer; and Mount Hood soars into the sky above the neighbouring state of Oregon.

History of eruption

Despite this density of great volcanoes in the north west of North America, there are only a few reports of eruptions. Until 1980, the volcanoes of the region were considered to be "alive" but not active. Today Mount St. Helens is classified as a dangerous volcano, yet until that day in May of 1980 reports of volcanic activity had been few. Evidence could be found for just four major eruptions over the last 520 years, each of which had ejected as much as 1 cubic km (1,308,000 cubic yards) of ash and stone, in addition to dozens of additional, smaller eruptions. In 1480 an eruption occured that by contemporary estimates was four times stronger than that of 1980. Impressive as that is, there are geological indications of even more violent activity during the approximately 50,000 years this powerful volcano has been in existence.

Lava bulge

A lava bulge is the result of many smaller eruptions. Its creation is comparable to an upright tube of toothpaste which squeezes out lava that is so rich in silicon and so viscous when cool that it can scarcely flow, if at all. At the upper, outer edge, the lava cools and a skin forms that tears from time to time when additional lava forces its way up from below. Occasionally small eruptions may occur, during which parts of the upper skin are catapulted into the air, due to greatly increased pressure inside the volcano. If the lava bulge inside the crater of Mount St. Helens were to continue to grow at its current rate of around 15 cubic km (3.6 cubic miles) a year, it would take almost a hundred years for the crater to refill itself to its level prior to the 1980 eruption.

In more recent times, there must have been an eruption in the year 1800. Missionaries, fur trappers and traders heard reports of clouds of ash and ash rain from Native Americans of the Sanspoil and Spokane tribes. In November 1842, the clergyman Josiah Parrish in Oregon, about 130 km (80 miles) south west of Mount St. Helens, witnessed an eruption. According to his report, the earth shook and ash rained down from a darkened sky. On the following day, Mount St. Helens had spread its ash over the Columbia River like a snow shower.

Mount St. Helens rising majestically above picturesque Spirit Lake.

The eruption of Vesusius

Among the most devestating volcano eruptions of all times is that of Vesusius on the Bay of Naples. In antiquity it was thought to be extinct, but in August of 79 CE it proved this to be entirely false. After a relatively small eruption, thousands of tons of dust and ashes were spewed into the sky anew and fell to the earth as a dense rain of ashes. At first large chunks fell, followed by fine, glowing hot ashes. Ships that approached the coast to help ran aground because the falling debris had actually raised the level of the sea floor. Ships could not leave the bay, either; all harbours were blocked. Flames blazed from the crater throughout the night, and before its fires were quenched the volcano eruption had destroyed Pompeii, Herculaneum and Stabiae, all cities built at the base of Vesuvius. It is estimated that over 17,000 people died in the fiery ashes. In the 1730s the ruins of the cities were discovered and excavations begun – making visible their suffering.

It is thought that there had been more or less continual volcanic activity at Mount St. Helens up until 1857. Thereafter, there were reports of smaller eruptions in 1898, 1903 and 1921, although there are no supporting records of these events. In light of what has become known since 1980, these must have been smaller eruptions or steam explosions with little ejection of rock. It is interesting to bear in mind that this region of the USA was only opened up to settlers at a very late point in US history. It was not until the second half of the nineteenth century that Oregon and Washington were first settled by Europeans; Oregon became a state in 1859 and Washington attained this status in 1889.

Settlement was extremely thin until the early 20th century. Thus it is not surprising that no exact details of volcanic activity prior to that time exist.

An earthquake triggers the catastrophe

Like most volcanoes of the Cascade Range, Mount St. Helens is a great cone filled with basalt, lava and other rocks. Several lava bulges had formed on its slopes prior to 1980.

The region around the volcano was a nature reserve, a paradise for hunters, anglers and hikers. Its thick woods, rich in fauna, as well as the trout and salmon that were plentiful in its streams and rivers, were an invitation to visitors.

During the two months prior to the catastrophic erup-

Dozens of square miles of woodland fell victim to the eruption and caught on fire.

The ashes preserved victims just as they were at the moment of death. The hollow spaces left in the ashes by bodies were filled with plaster, resulting in dramatic statues.

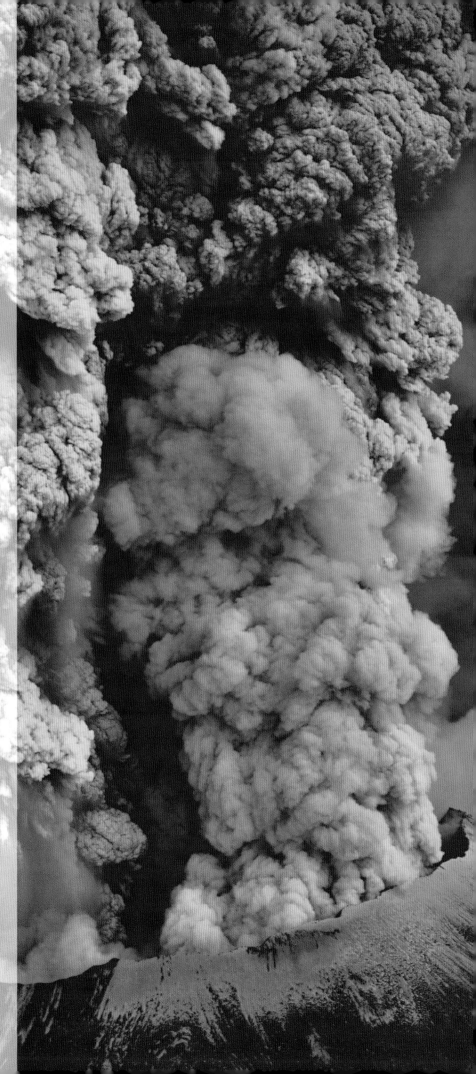

tion more than 10,000 earthquakes were registered in the state of Washington, including several steam explosions. At the same time, the swelling of the lava bulge on the north flank, known as Goat Rocks, increased by more than 80 m (262 ft).

On 18 May, at 8:32 a.m., an earthquake of magnitude 5.1 occured directly under the volcano. This was the trigger for the enormous eruption that quickly followed in its wake. Within a few seconds the entire north flank of the moutain had exploded, creating one of the most gargantuan rock and debris avalanches of all time, advancing at a speed of 100 km/60 miles per hour. Within seconds, the temperature in the danger zone soared to over 300°C/570°F. Snow and ice on the peak of Mount St. Helens melted, creating raging torrents that poured down the slopes into the valleys, destroying all life in their path. Within minutes, a cloud of ash formed over the volcano that rose more than 19 km (11 miles) upwards. The wind blew nearly 600 million tons of ash over almost 60,000 square km (23,000 square miles) of the north western USA. By lunchtime the ash cloud in the stratosphere had reached the state of Idaho to the east, and by 3:00 p.m. it reached Montana, from where the prevailing winds started to move it towards the south. At the end of the day, it had arrived in Colorado to the south east. On this day, the volcano lost significant height: within a few hours the peak of the mountain, now missing, was transformed into ash and dust that lay over the north western USA like a blanket. Witnesses in various states described the explosion as deafening, and the ash rain as a fine grey sand that smelled of sulphur.

Since the 1980 eruption, a new lava bulge measuring 250 m (820 ft) high and 1,100 m (3,600 ft) in diameter has formed. It is estimated to contain around 90 million cubic m (3,200 million cubic ft) of lava.

Fifty-seven people lost their lives as a direct result of the catastrophe. The eruption was also indirectly responsible for a further seven victims in a plane crash and a severe motor accident, thus establishing the total number of fatalities as sixty-four.

Smoke and ash were catapulted out of Mount St. Helens in Washington state by the massive eruption of 18 May 1980.

The worst ever chemical industrial disaster took place at the Union Carbide factory in Bhopal, India in the early hours of 3 December 1984.

1984

A DEADLY CLOUD AT MIDNIGHT

THE BHOPAL DISASTER

Just after midnight on 3 December 1984, the most extreme industrial accident of all time released a poison cloud of chemical gas in the Indian provincial capital of Bhopal. A tank in a pesticide plant operated by the Union Carbide Company released 40 tons of methylisocyanat (MIC) into the atmosphere after automatically opening its safety ventilators in response to a sudden increase in internal pressure. The weight of the chemical compound means that the poisonous cloud cannot dissipate. Instead, it rolled across the city at ground level, bringing suffering and death to every household. Over 3,800 people died immediately, with hundreds of thousands gravely injured. The scope of the tragedy is still difficult to comprehend today, with many of those affected still awaiting compensation.

The American chemical industry invests in India

Bhopal is the capital of the province of Mahya Pradesh located in central India. It is an industrial city with a university and over 1.5 million inhabitants, though at the time of the disaster the population was about half its current level. The chemical industry is the region's largest

Eyewitness account
"People were desperate to save their lives so they just ran. Those who fell were not picked up by anybody, they were trampled by other people. Even cows were running to save their lives, crushing people as they ran."
Champa Devi Shukla, leader of the Bhopal victims' rights movement

employer. In 1934 Union Carbide Corporation (UCC) was one of the first American investors in India when it formed the highly profitable Union Carbide India Limited (UCIL). The chemical plant in Bhopal, which was built in the 1970s, employed 9,000 people. In 1984 UCC reported profits of $9.5 billion, making it the largest chemical firm in the world.

Poison gas rolls into residential areas

It all ended tragically shortly after midnight on 3 December 1984 when methylisocyanat (MIC) was released into the atmosphere. Controversial studies have determined that 3,828 people died at once, and hundreds of thousands were overcome by the gas. The next day, Warren Anderson, president of Union Carbide, arrived from Connecticut accompanied by a rescue team. Upon his arrival in India, however, the government placed him under house arrest with orders to leave the country within 24 hours. Nonetheless, Union Carbide remained long enough to organize medical and technical rescue squads, working together with local aid agencies in Bhopal.

Of the 500,000 people exposed to the gas, around one-fifth still suffer the after-effects in the form of chronic or incurable illnesses. Many have been blinded, and the cancer rate among survivors is well above average. In addition, more than two decades after the catastrophe, every fourth pregnancy in Bhopal ends in stillbirth. Over the years, Union Carbide has reluctantly paid out $690 million in reparations, of which it is said only a small part reaches the actual victims owing to government corruption.

How the accident happened

MIC had been manufactured in the Bhopal plant only since 1979. Prior to that, it had been imported from the United States. Workers were the first to smell the MIC on 3 December, and they began to search for a possible leak in one of the holding tanks. In the course of mere minutes, the temperature and pressure in tank 610 climbed to such a high level that the safety mechanisms kicked in and began to release the gas into the atmosphere. About 24 tons of MIC and 12 tons of other toxic compounds formed a deadly cloud that settled close to the ground. Within seconds it began to roll slowly towards the residential part of the city.

Subsequent investigations showed that the tank pressure had increased after water was introduced into the mixture of chemicals. There are three possible ways that this could have happened. The tank may have been rinsed out, but not properly dried before use. Sabotage, perhaps by a disgruntled worker, is another possibility (a water hose from elsewhere in the plant was found attached to one of the MIC tank's regulating meters). Finally, it is possible that the workers looking for the leak introduced water into the tank in error.

Old and inadequate technology

In 1984, there were 37 public telephones in the entire city of Bhopal, only two of which were capable of dialing long distance. This gives some

The afflicted residential quarter collapsed into chaos as the cloud of poison gas drifted close to the ground through the narrow streets and alleys.

In the years leading up to the incident, Union Carbide had shut down many divisions of the Bhopal plant because they were less profitable than expected. Restructuring led to large parts of the complex being closed or left operating with equipment that had not been properly maintained. This was the situation on the day of the accident. Inadequate technological support gravely affected the safety systems. For a place where dangerous chemicals were handled daily, the emergency procedures were woefully inadequate. In addition, a recent mass lay-off of skilled workers and foremen had led to a dearth of experience at all levels. The new managers had, for the most part, no experience in the chemical industry. In addition, the atmosphere inside the plant had been troubled even before 3 December. Many small acts of sabotage had recently been discovered.

The conclusion of many investigating bodies was that given the conditions inside the plant and in the city of Bhopal, almost any accident would have quickly developed into a catastrophic disaster of comparable proportions. The director of the chemical plant was arrested and a warrant was issued for Union Carbide president Warren Anderson on a charge of negligent homicide.

The 20th anniversary of the Bhopal disaster was commemorated on 12 February 2004. Activists estimate the death toll at 33,000.

sense of the paucity of infrastructure in the area at the time of the disaster, a lack that had tragic consequences in the face of a catastrophe of this magnitude. The local population, mostly poor and uneducated, had never been given any information about the plant or the risks involved in the production of chemical pesticides. No one knew what to do in case of any accident, let alone one of this magnitude. If people had known that the best reaction to a toxic cloud is to lie flat on the ground with a wet cloth over their face, many lives could have been spared. Instead, people ran around in blind panic. Physical exertion led them to inhale more of the poisonous gases, and more deeply, than if they had simply lain down on the ground and waited for it to pass.

People continue to suffer and die

The aftermath has been horrific. Union Carbide and the new owner of the plant, Dow Chemical,

Methylisocyanat (MIC)

Methylisocyanat is a highly flammable, colourless liquid with a pungent aroma. Among other applications, it is commonly used in insect sprays. When MIC comes in contact with water and heat, the compound breaks down into the toxic gases cyanide and nitrous oxide, both of which are also highly explosive. MIC is categorized as a contact poison capable of breaking down into its component gases at temperatures as low as 20 °C (68°F). When inhaled or otherwise in contact with a person or animal, the skin, respiratory system, and eyes become severely inflamed; the eyes are usually most severely affected. MIC can burn away the corneal tissue, leading to vision impairment and blindness. When the chemicals enter the body itself, nausea, vomiting, abdominal cramps, and severe sore throat are the initial symptoms. Dizziness and loss of consciousness can result. In the worst cases, a toxic build up of fluid in the lungs (oedema) leads to death. MIC affects all mammals, making its introduction into the environment potentially catastrophic.

have never released precise information regarding the components of the toxic cloud, claiming these are industry secrets. As a result, the victims do not know the exact poisons to which they were exposed, nor in what concentration. This lack of knowledge keeps doctors from providing appropriate medical care. The international environmental watchdog organization Greenpeace published reports on the Bhopal disaster in 1999 and 2002. They claim that the area around the factory is thoroughly contaminated with heavy metal residue and other toxic substances. Dow Chemical nevertheless has no plans for decontamination. The profits from the Bhopal plant are declining and the costs of cleanup too high. In the meantime, the chemicals have found their way into the local drinking water. During the dry season, the contaminated dust blows the toxic substances into the air, far and wide. In Bhopal, children born with birth defects are a regular occurrence. The British medical journal *Lancet* catalogued statistical increases for a wide range of birth defects, including cleft palate, three eyes, webbed fingers, extra fingers, one testicle instead of two, irregular skull shape and Down's syndrome.

As you read this, people continue to suffer and die in Bhopal as a result of the 1984 disaster.

Women wearing masks demonstrate in Bhopal in 2002, demanding that Union Carbide president Warren Anderson be brought to trial for homicide.

2,500 foetuses stillborn after the Bhopal disaster are stored at the Gandhi Medical College in India.

Extracts from a 2005 statement by the Union Carbide Corporation (UCC)

The 1984 gas leak in Bhopal was a terrible tragedy that understandably continues to evoke strong emotions even 22 years later. In the wake of the gas release, Union Carbide Corporation, and then-chairman Warren Anderson, worked diligently to provide aid to the victims and set up a process to resolve their claims.

Shortly after the gas release, Union Carbide launched an aggressive effort to identify the cause. The engineering consulting firm Arthur D. Little, Inc. conducted a thorough investigation. Its conclusion: the gas leak could only have been caused by deliberate sabotage. Someone purposely put water in the gas storage tank, and this caused a massive chemical reaction. Process safety systems had been put in place that would have kept the water from entering into the tank by accident.

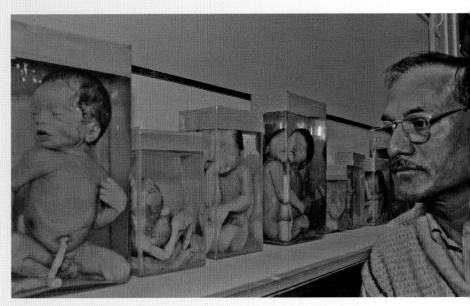

Challenger lifting off at the Kennedy Space Center in Cape Canaveral, Florida.

1986

A BALL OF FIRE

THE EXPLOSION OF THE CHALLENGER SPACE SHUTTLE

Challenger, NASA's second space shuttle for outer space operations, completed its maiden flight in 1983. In its three-year history *Challenger* made ten space flights, spending a total of 69 days in outer space and orbiting the earth 987 times. Among its successes were the deployment of the first tracking and communications satellite and the testing of a new NASA space shuttle suit. Then came 28 January 1986, the day of the *Challenger* catastrophe: 73 seconds after a perfect launch for mission STS-51-L, *Challenger* exploded, killing six astronauts and one civilian.

Challenger's historic contributions to space travel

The space shuttle was named after the US Navy research ship *Challenger*, which was seen as its forerunner. Previously, the *Apollo 17* lunar module had also been named *Challenger*. Prior

A whole country in mourning
"We will never forget them, nor the last time we saw them, this morning, as they prepared for their journey and waved goodbye and slipped the surly bonds of Earth to touch the face of God."

Ronald Reagan, US President 1981–1989, quoting John Gillespie Magee's poem *High Flight*.

to the tragic accident, the orbiter had completed ten flights without incident. In fact, this spacecraft had been involved in several milestones in the development of American space travel: in 1983 Sally Ride was the first American female astronaut in outer space; in a separate mission that year, Guy S. Bluford was the first African-American astronaut in space; and in February 1984, Bruce McCandless II performed the first manoeuvre outside the shuttle (EVA, or extra-vehicular activity) without a safety line, moving about 30 m (100 ft) away from the space-craft. The *Challenger* was the world's first space shuttle to land safely at the Kennedy Space Center in Florida, and also made the first successful launch and landing by night. In the course of three flights in 1985, *Challenger* sent the Spacelab station into orbit, which provided an environment for a great number of tests, including experiments with live animals. On yet another mission, *Challenger* transported the European Space Agency's Spacelab-3. During its last flight, this utterly successful space shuttle had a civilian on board for the first time in the history of space travel: a woman named Christa McAuliffe, a teacher from New Hampshire. The plan was for her to teach school children from outer space.

A class from outer space

Over the years, the public had increasingly come to question the benefits of the NASA space missions. The quest for manned space

travel devoured billions of dollars, and its original purpose had been nothing more than to get a head start in the Cold War. During the mid-1980s, the popularity of the space program hit an all-time low. People were hardly following the launches and landings of the spacecrafts anymore. In an attempt to revive the popularity of the NASA research program (and to secure further government funding), the expensive space program was elevated to the level of a pop media event.

One effective promotional idea was to send the "girl next door" into outer space. For the Teacher in Space program thus devised, 37-year-old Christa McAuliffe, teacher and mother of two, was chosen from among 11,500 applicants to become an astronaut. At the same time, American school children were told they would experience the future and be taught directly from outer space. The plan worked. Millions of American classrooms took part – but as fate would have it, they did not sit in on a class taught from outer space. Instead, they experienced the tragedy live on TV, and many required psychological counselling in the after-

The Challenger crew. From left to right, back: Ellison S. Onizuka, Christa McAuliffe, Gregory Jarvis, Judith A. Resnik; front: Michael J. Smith, Francis R. Scobee and Ronald E. McNair.

On 28 January 1986, within 73 seconds of lift-off, millions of television viewers around the world witnessed the dramatic disintegration of the Challenger.

math of the catastrophe: 73 seconds after what appeared to be a picture-perfect launch, viewers around the world watched in horror as the *Challenger* disintegrated.

Investigation of the catastrophe

After the accident, then President Ronald Reagan (1911–2004) established the Rogers Commission to investigate its causes. As is customary in the aftermath of fatal catastrophes, a quest was begun to find the one factor that could explain the unfathomable. As early as six months after the tragedy, the first reports were available. It emerged that brittle O-rings on the shuttle's right solid rocket booster caused the disaster. It also became clear that NASA ignored several safety measures, as well as the warnings of experts about those very O-rings. The countdown had started and it was not going to be halted.

It is now clear that *Challenger* should never have launched on that January morning in 1986 because there was a frost that day at Cape Canaveral. It has been shown that the unusual cold, in connection with the sudden increase in

heat caused by ignition of the engines, made the booster's rubber O-rings brittle, and this led to leakage. Photographs show trails of smoke being emitted from the shuttle even before lift-off. With the decision to launch, the fate of Richard Scobee, Michael Smith, Judith Resnik, Ellison Onizuka, Ronald McNair, Gregory Jarvis and Christa McAuliffe was sealed at the time of lift-off. The leak increased rapidly, and within seconds sparks impinged on the main tank. After a few more seconds, the tank caught fire, and the 1.4 million litres (308,000 gallons) of hydrogen and oxygen in the shuttle's tank exploded.

The debris was scattered over large parts of Florida's east coast. For months, NASA divers actively recovered parts of the shuttle from the ocean. It was another two months before, in March 1986, they succeeded in recovering the cockpit with the remains of the crew. Analysis of the cockpit demonstrated that the seven passengers survived the initial explosion: at least three of them had made use of the emergency oxygen system to breathe. It seems that they fell from a height of 17 km (10.5 miles) for 3 minutes – quite possibly fully conscious – before hitting the surface of the Atlantic Ocean with unimagineable force.

The consequences

As a consequence of the *Challenger* accident and the Rogers Commission's report, government authorities suspended further shuttle flights. It would be more than two and a half years before *Discovery*, the next shuttle, was launched on 29 September 1988. More than 2,000 improvements had to be made before NASA was allowed to resume space travel. The solid rocket booster that caused the *Challenger* disaster was completely revised, and the cockpit now features an emergency exit, making it necessary for astronauts to go back to wearing pressure suits in order to guarantee they have a sufficient amount of air to breathe during launch and landing. NASA abandoned the practice of sending satellites into orbit with manned spacecrafts, and now uses unmanned satellite launchers instead. In 1991, *Endeavour*, the best space shuttle to date, was completed, and NASA experienced no further losses for several years – until the next tragedy occured in January 2003, when the space shuttle *Columbia* exploded during a landing manoeuvre, killing all seven crew members.

The space shuttle Challenger with open cargo doors, orbiting the earth.

Crew members of the USS Preserver recover a large section of the ruptured Challenger from the depths of the ocean off the coast of Florida.

Destroyed reactor #4 was encased in a "sarcophagus" of iron and concrete that, over time, has begun to disintegrate. Not until 2001 could technicians shut down all the reactor blocks in the Chernobyl nuclear power plant.

1986

NUCLEAR MELTDOWN

THE CHERNOBYL DISASTER

In the early hours of 26 April 1986, one of four reactors in the Chernobyl nuclear power plant in the Ukraine exploded. The threat that opponents of peaceful uses of nuclear power have always warned against had become reality: nuclear meltdown. The radioactive materials set free by the explosion were spread over a wide area by the heat from the burning complex, and a toxic cloud climbed more than 1,700 m (5,600 ft) into the sky. Over the next several days, this atomic cloud drifted over most of Europe. The long-term health effects, which are still being investigated today, will continue to be a factor for many generations to come.

A deadly test

On 25 April 1986, arrangements were made for a series of experiments to be conducted in reactor block #4 of the Chernobyl nuclear power plant. The goal was to determine what would happen in case of a complete loss of electricity. Would the power plant's turbines contain enough residual electricity to keep the cooling system running until power could be restored? In order to conduct the test under the most realistic conditions possible, all emergency control systems were turned off. The test was delayed, however, by unexpected local power requirements during the afternoon and evening. This meant that it had to be carried out much later than originally planned, and by night shift workers who were poorly prepared for the task.

Some families voluntarily remained in their home villages located within the 30-km (18.5-mile) restricted zone.

A series of operational errors led to the reaction rate in block #4 increasing until it got out of control. Staff wanted to end the experiment, but the power plant's interim chief engineer ordered them to continue. By the time the emergency control system was finally reactivated manually at 1:23 a.m. it was too late. Key components had melted in the extreme heat generated during the test and it was no longer possible to stop the reactor. A few minutes later, an enormous explosion of steam blew the 3,000-ton roof off reactor block #4. The 1,500 tons of radioactive graphite inside the reactor ignited in a fiery holocaust. The fire drove radioactive particles so high into the atmosphere that they could be detected thousands of miles above the earth's surface.

Late reaction

On 27 and 29 April 1986, scientists in Finland and Sweden reported higher than normal levels of atmospheric radiation. Since they had no information as to its cause, they immediately launched an investigation of Swedish nuclear plants to search for damage. Not until late in the evening of 28 April did the Soviet Union announce that there had been an accident involving a nuclear core meltdown in a reactor 100 km (62 miles) north of Kiev. Inhabitants of the Chernobyl region received this news at the same time as the international community: until that point, they had had no idea what was happening.

This computer simulation shows the extent of the radioactive cloud on the day of the disaster.

Evacuation of the inhabitants of the affected areas began some 36 hours after the explosion. The 50,000 inhabitants of the city of Pripiat, only 3 km (1.9 miles) from the power plant, were transported out of the danger zone by an enormous fleet of buses. In the weeks that followed, 67,000 people would be evacuated. A restricted zone 30 km (18.5 miles) in diameter is currently in place around the reactor site, and Pripiat is an abandoned ghost town.

The Liquidators

In order to put a halt to the immediate after effects of the accident, the fire in the destroyed reactor had to be extinguished and the exposed radioactive material encased. A number of workers were brought in, many of whom had little idea of the danger they were being exposed to. This group, later known as the Liquidators, consisted primarily of young men fulfilling

As late as 1990, animals were still being born with serious defects in the region around Chernobyl. Most lived only a few hours.

Reactor blocks #1 and #2 at Chernobyl were back in operation as early as November 1986. Workers were brought to the power plant in special buses.

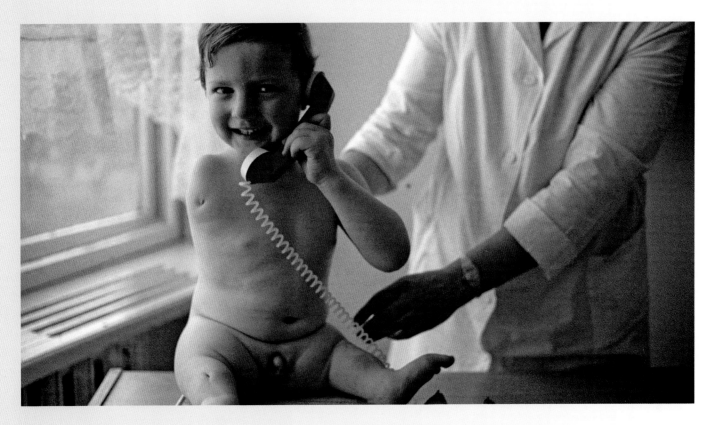

their military service obligation, reservists, students and miners. Although the exact number of Liquidators remains unknown, it is estimated that as many as one million men were involved in the project through the early 1990s. The government officially recognizes only 60,000, all of whom are entitled to receive free medical care based on their service at Chernobyl. At least 50,000 workers have died of conditions caused by working in reactor block #4. Twenty years after the disaster, experts calculate that 500,000 people have died from the direct or indirect effects of the explosion and meltdown. The official government report, however, recognizes only 4,000 victims.

This photo of a Chernobyl child was published around the world. The boy was later adopted by a British family.

Chernobyl AIDS

From the very first days after the accident it was feared that leukaemia and thyroid cancer would be on the rise for decades after the disaster. Twenty years after the rain of radioactive material, studies show that cancer rates are as much as 50 times higher than normal. An even bigger problem has been widespread immune deficiency among children in the affected areas. This phenomenon, called Chernobyl AIDS, has been the subject of increasing attention. Affected children are so debilitated that their bodies are virtually incapable of fighting off illness. They are chronically fatigued, lack the ability to concentrate for more than a few minutes, and suffer from many psychological conditions. Diseases affecting the respiratory, digestive, skeletal and muscle systems are on also the rise.

The Liquidators should have been outfitted with heavy protective clothing. However, in the early days after the accident, this seldom happened.

1994

A COLD DEATH
IN THE BALTIC SEA

THE UNSOLVED SINKING OF THE ESTONIA

In the early hours of 28 September 1994, the automobile and passenger ferry *Estonia* sank in a stormy Baltic Sea. Eight hundred fifty-two people perished in what came to be known as the greatest ship disaster in post-war European history. The ferry was travelling her regular route from Tallinn, Estonia to Stockholm, Sweden. Officially, the *Estonia*'s bow door broke off, and the subsequent inrush of water sank her. Even today, however, speculations abound that the actual causes of the catastrophe have been obscured.

The last voyage

On the evening of 27 September 1994, the cruise ferry *Estonia* was loaded in the harbour of the Estonian capital, Tallinn. Her destination was Stockholm, the Swedish capital, and the scheduled travelling time was approximately 15 hours. The ferry was only half booked on that day: the documentation records 803 passengers, 186 crew members, and 100 vehicles.

Two months after the Estonia sank, her bow door was salvaged from the bottom of the sea.

One of the survivors later reported that the harbour had been locked down immediately prior to the ferry's departure, and that two sizeable trailer trucks, escorted by a military convoy, were directed towards the ship. According to this survivor's account, the loading ramp and the ship's bow door were only closed after those trucks had been unloaded. The *Estonia* departed on her last voyage at 7:15 p.m., about 15 minutes behind schedule.

The sinking

The Baltic Sea was rough and ice-cold on that fall night. The waves were 4–6 m (13–20 ft) high, and the water temperature was no more than a chilly 12 °C/50°F. After midnight, the *Estonia* began to pitch violently, with waves crashing over her bow. At about 0:45 a.m., passengers heard thuds and noises that differed markedly from the relatively constant sound of breakers crashing against the ship. Within half an hour, so much water had entered the ship that she tilted at a 25° angle. It appears that the ferry's bow visor had broken off, and the loading ramp behind the visor – designed to function as a safety barrier – could not prevent the inrush of water. At 1:22 a.m., the ship sent out the first Mayday call, and the onboard alarm called the crew to man the lifeboat stations. When the second Mayday call went out two minutes later, however, the *Estonia* was already listing at an angle of 45°, making it nearly impossible to move about the ship and reach the lifeboats. From that point on, the catastrophe rapidly ran its course. By 1:48 a.m., *Estonia* had already disappeared from radar screens: she had sunk into the icy cold waters of the 80-m (260-ft) deep Baltic Sea.

A hopeless rescue operation

The Baltic Sea has a relatively high frequency of shipping traffic, and 11 ships heard the second distress call sounded by the *Estonia*. Rescue operations began at once. About an hour after the sinking, the first ships arrived at the scene of the accident – but even that brief period was too long to survive in the cold sea. Many passengers who were able to abandon ship in time succumbed to hypothermia either in the water itself or in the cold winds aboard

The Estonia
The Estonia *was built in 1980 at the Meyer-Werft shipyard in Papenburg, Germany. For her first 12 years, under the names* Viking Sally, Silja Star *and* Wasa King, *she served various ocean carriers on the Baltic Sea. From 1992 onwards she was in operation for a joint Swedish-Estonian venture, cruising between Tallinn and Stockholm under the name* Estonia. *At the time, the ferry was the largest and most modern ship operating under the Estonian flag. She was a RORO ferry (roll-on/roll-off), allowing vehicles to drive onto the cargo decks through massive bow and stern doors and leave the ship without having to reverse. Since there are no bulkheads between the cargo decks, any inrush of water would immediately lead to* dangerous listing. *Because of this safety hazard, the* Estonia *was supposed to serve only in safe waters and on short distances of no more than 37 km (23 miles). Regulating authorities, however, had tolerated the* Estonia's *use on significantly longer routes for 14 years.*

the life rafts. Most of the passengers, however, were not able to leave the rapidly sinking ship in the first place; they were dragged to the bottom of the sea along with the ferry. No fewer than 852 people lost their lives, making the

Survivors of the catastrophe were rescued and flown to nearby hospitals by Navy rescue helicopters.

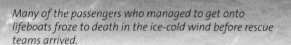

*Many of the passengers who managed to get onto
lifeboats froze to death in the ice-cold wind before rescue
teams arrived.*

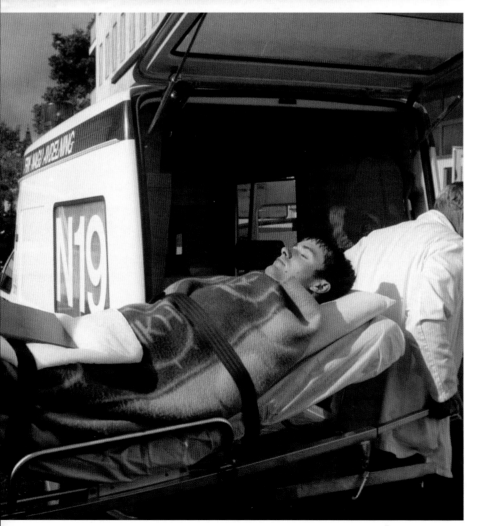

Estonia accident the deadliest maritime disaster
in post-war European history. Only 137 people
managed to survive the catastrophe.

Curious inconsistencies

Soon after the accident, an official commission
investigated the causes and details of the catastrophe. The commission's conclusions boiled
down to an unfortunate combination of constructional flaws and stormy weather. In an
attempt to mount a defence against the charges
of constructional flaws, Meyer-Werft tried to
perform their own analysis, only to discover
that important evidence was withheld from
independent investigators. It is also worthy of
note that the Swedish government commis-
sioned a Dutch company specializing in the
neutralization of underwater nuclear waste to
seal the wreck in a concrete sarcophagus. This
procedure would have made any future investigations impossible; however, it was never
carried out.

The rampant rumours about the *Estonia*
transporting secret military equipment could
neither be proven nor convincingly rebutted. In

*Only 137 of almost 1,000 people aboard the ferry survived
this accident, making the sinking of the Estonia the most
severe ship catastrophe in European post-war history.*

September 2004, a Swedish TV broadcaster ran a report in which a retired Swedish customs officer claimed that the *Estonia* was, in fact, used for secret transports of Soviet military technology to the West, and that customs officers had been given orders to let certain vehicles pass without checking, even though all other vehicles boarding the *Estonia* were inspected in great detail. Another thread that fuels the conspiracy theories concerns a mysterious black suitcase that rescue divers allegedly sought in the wreck. The existence of such a suitcase was later denied.

The survivors who vanished

Perhaps most disturbing of all, some relatives of those who died in the *Estonia* accident claimed that they received messages after the catastrophe stating that their spouses or children had survived the accident. Some survivors also confirm that the twins Hannely and Hannika Veide, for example, were able to board a lifeboat; the Swedish rescue headquarters also has the twins listed among the survivors. They are among a group of people who, disturbingly, were initially recorded as survivors, but seem to have disappeared without a trace at some later point in time.

In March 2006, a report by a new commission of inquiry was published that cast further doubt on the first commission's final and official report. The true causes of the catastrophe seem to be unclear to this day.

This map illustrates the Estonia's route across the Baltic Sea. The circle indicates where the ferry sank.

The *Herald of Free Enterprise*

Another terrible ferry accident occurred on 6 March 1987. On the evening of that day, 459 passengers and 80 crew members were on board the cross-channel ferry Herald of Free Enterprise. It was carrying 81 cars, 3 buses and 47 trucks. When the ferry left the port of Zeebrugge, Belgium, its bow doors were left open as usual in order to let the exhaust gases escape. Just before the harbour's exit, the ferry turned and started travelling forward at full speed. This would have been the time for the officer in charge to close the bow doors, but he was on a break and asleep in his cabin at the time. The bow doors were not visible from the bridge, and there was no control light that allowed the captain to verify their status from the bridge, which would have helped prevent the accident (and has since become mandatory). While the ferry was accelerating to full speed, the tragedy unfolded very rapidly. Water entered through the open bow doors, and the ship capsized onto a sand bank just 20 minutes after her departure. Although rescue operations were initiated immediately, 193 people died in the 3°C/37°F cold waters of the English Channel.

THE DEMISE OF A SYMBOL OF PEACE

CONCORDE BURSTS INTO FLAMES

On 25 July 2000, Air France Flight 4590 from Charles de Gaulle International Airport in Paris en route to John F. Kennedy Airport in New York crashed just minutes after take-off. Concorde was the only supersonic passenger aircraft in the history of Western aviation and a "symbol of peace and international understanding" (Tony Benn, then British Minister of Technology). When it burst into flames, all 113 people aboard lost their lives.

The engines on Concorde's left wing caught fire just after take-off. The catastrophe was caused by a burst tyre.

The safest passenger aircraft in history

Concorde was a joint development by Britain and France beginning in the late 1950s. Its top speed was twice the speed of sound, a phenomenal 2,200 km/1,360 miles per hour. The first prototype took its maiden flights in the spring of 1969, and commercial operations began in 1976. To this day, Concorde remains the only Western supersonic aeroplane to have been used for regular air traffic. Concorde was considered the safest plane in the world, a reputation based on its ratio of air miles to passenger deaths (zero). While the Boeing 737 fleet taken as a whole travels more passenger miles each week and logs more flight hours than Concorde did in its entire history, this is due to the number of Boeing aircraft and their extensive flight network.

A titanium strip on the runway

On that summer day in July 2000, Concorde was scheduled to fly from Charles de Gaulle airport in Paris to New York. The trouble began even before take-off when Concorde, which had already accelerated to a speed of 300 km/ 185 miles per hour, ran over a 40-cm (15-in) titanium strip that was lying on the runway. This strip originated from an American Continental Airlines DC10 that had taken off from the same runway four minutes earlier. The affected Concorde tyre burst, and a large chunk of it hit the underside of the plane's left wing with such strong force that it damaged one of the fuel tanks. The leaking fuel ignited instantaneously, either due to a spark from electrical

wiring or due to contact with some of the extremely hot parts of the engine. Moments later, as the plane was taking off, engines 1 and 2 simultaneously lost all power, but recovered during the following seconds. When a fire erupted in engine 2, flames trailed behind the plane in long streams, and the crew switched off the engine in response to a fire warning generated by an on-board computer. At this point, the pilot had no choice but to continue the start manoeuvre. He planned to fly to the nearby Le Bourget airport and attempt an emergency landing there.

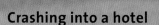

Crashing into a hotel

With only three of the four engines functioning properly, however, and the damaged landing gear impossible to retract, Concorde was not able to gain speed or altitude: at an elevation of merely 60 m (200 ft), the plane was flying at 370 km/230 miles per hour rather than the 400 km/250 miles per hour necessary for take-off and ascent. Engine 1 caught fire, causing it to fail as well, leaving the plane powered only by engines 3 and 4. This resulted in asymmetric thrust, which lifted the right wing and rolled

Concorde crashed into a hotel near the airport, killing four hotel guests.

Concern about further accidents

"The accident of 25 July shows that the destruction of a tyre (an event that we cannot say will not recur) had catastrophic consequences within moments, preventing the crew from rectifying the situation."

French Air Accident
Investigation Bureau (BEA)

the plane into a 100-degree bank. In an attempt to bring the aircraft back to a level position, the pilot was forced to reduce power in the remaining engines – but this reduced the airspeed further still and he lost control of the plane. Tragically, Concorde crashed into *Les Relais Bleus*, a hotel in Gonesse, near the airport. All nine crew members, all one hundred passengers on board and four people on the ground lost their lives.

All Concorde flights stopped

A few days after the accident, all Concorde flights were grounded until the International Aviation Safety Agency could thoroughly investigate the accident and make recommendations. One Air France aircraft located in New York at the time was allowed to fly back to Paris, although without passengers. In addition to investigating the causes of the accident, the

The firefighters could do no more than extinguish Concorde's burning wreckage. None of the crew or passengers could be rescued.

Records by Concorde

In its time, Concorde set several records: in 1995, it took off from Paris and flew around the globe to return to its airport of departure in 32 hours, 27 minutes and 49 seconds, including all intermediate stops. On 7 February 1996, a British Airways Concorde set a world record of 2 hours, 52 minutes and 59 seconds between New York and London. In August 1999, during a total eclipse of the sun, three Concorde aircraft crossed the Atlantic Ocean, flying along with the shadow of the moon at Mach 2. The 300 passengers on board experienced the eclipse three to four times longer than observers on the ground.

A British Airways Concorde during take-off from John F. Kennedy International Airport. The flight to London Heathrow Airport on 26 July 2000, one day after the crash, took place without any passengers.

The wrecked aircraft left a scene of devastation and cost Air France millions in damages. In addition to being ordered to pay large sums in compensation, the company suffered tremendous losses while all Concordes were grounded, pending the investigation results.

agency also invited proposals on how to improve the Concorde fleet. Analyses showed the need for a few changes; above all, they were to be equipped with tyres developed specially for Concorde planes that could not burst.

Long-standing problems with the tyres

It was not until 2005 that French authorities initiated proceedings against Continental Airlines on the basis of their use of the titanium strip that was lying on the runway, which was not actually approved (it had been used by the airline because titanium is more robust than traditional metals). In the same year, Jacques Herubel, a former flight engineer, came under

investigation. It had come to light that there had been more than 70 incidents involving the tyres on Concorde between 1979 and 2000, but Herubel, the flight engineer in charge, had neglected the issue and failed to take steps to correct known defects.

When the identified defects had been corrected, test flights were conducted in July 2001 and the Concorde was actually in flight once again on 11 September 2001, when the terrorist attacks on the World Trade Center in New York City took place. As an indirect consequence, transatlantic air traffic dwindled. With passenger numbers dropping, Concorde service became less profitable and was ultimately discontinued in 2003.

Concorde, the only Western supersonic aircraft ever operated in regular air traffic, was considered the safest aeroplane until the Paris tragedy.

71

THE PRIDE OF THE RUSSIAN NAVY SINKS

THE NUCLEAR SUBMARINE KURSK EXPLODES

On 12 August 2000, the front section of the Russian nuclear submarine *Kursk* was completely destroyed by an explosion. A torpedo that had been readied for firing caught fire and exploded while still inside the boat. Of 118 crew members, only 23 survived the first minutes of the catastrophe. While the world continued for several days to hope for a miraculous rescue of these survivors, it later turned out that only four hours after the accident, even those sailors had no chance of surviving. The pride of the Russian Navy sank to the bottom of the Barents Sea, claiming 118 lives.

Fleet manoeuvre

The Kursk was part of a naval unit within the Russian Northern Fleet. In August 2000, that unit participated in a manoeuvre in the Barents Sea.

On 9 August 2000, the Russian Northern Fleet set out for a manoeuvre in the Barents Sea, part of the Arctic Ocean. The exercise, during which new weapons were to be tested, involved some 30 battleships, including the heavy missile cruiser *Peter the Great*, the aircraft carrier *Admiral Kuznetsov*, and the pride of the Russian Navy, the nuclear submarine *Kursk*. With a length of 150 m (492 ft), the *Kursk* was twice as long as a jumbo jet. The gigantic submarine had the reputation of being unsinkable; it was said that not even a direct hit could destroy her. 12 August was expected to be a great day for the *Kursk*: the plan was to test a new, top-secret torpedo. For this reason, a number of distinguished guests were on board, including five high-ranking officers of the fleet's command. Since one of the *Kursk*'s functions was to destroy enemy aircraft carriers, she also carried guided cruise missiles with 700-kg (1500-lb) warheads.

Underwater explosion

Four minutes prior to the explosion, the *Kursk* radio operator requested permission to fire from the Northern Fleet commander on board the missile cruiser *Peter the Great*. Permission was granted, and the commander of the *Kursk* issued the command.

At 9:30 a.m. CEST, Norwegian seismologists registered two explosions in the vicinity of the manoeuvre, about 180 km (112 miles) northeast of the Russian seaport of Murmansk. Something had evidently gone wrong when the torpedo was fired. The missile may have had a constructional flaw, or the torpedo hatch may

The Kursk in her home port in Vidyayevo on the Kola Peninsula, a few months before she sank.

not have opened properly. The missile's fuel exploded, killing seven seamen in the torpedo station compartment instantly. The commander immediately gave his final orders: to empty the ballast tanks and prepare for an emergency evacuation. Within a minute of the explosion, the submarine started surfacing at full speed, but no further orders were issued from the command centre. Meanwhile, the raging, enormously hot fire in the torpedo compartment triggered the explosion of the torpedo's warhead. An explosion equivalent to 1 ton of TNT blasted away the entire forecastle. The shock wave of the explosion tore through the submarine with enormous force, killing the 79 members of the crew in the first four compartments, including all seamen on the bridge and in the radio room. Only the compartment containing the propulsion reactor was protected by a massive steel wall.

The Kursk was not reported as missing

At that point, the *Kursk* ceased to surface and instead began to sink rapidly towards the bottom of the sea. Three minutes after the explosion, she crashed onto the seabed, and more members of the crew died on impact. When the reactors shut down automatically, leaving the submarine lying immobilized under the sea, only 23 seamen were still alive. The survivors crawled to the back of the boat, where the remaining air had accumulated. The air, however, was so toxic that they could only survive wearing protection suits, which supplied air for up to four hours. When the emergency batteries failed, the ship went dark.

Divers prepare to investigate the sunken wreck of the Kursk.

On 30 July 2000, about four weeks before the catastrophe, the Kursk participated in a fleet parade.

Above the water's surface, it seems that nobody noticed the catastrophe. Since the *Kursk* had been scheduled to remain submerged for another 3 hours, she was not missed, and no search and rescue operation was initiated. About 4 hours after the first explosion, the remaining 23 survivors were dead, as well. Not one of the 118 people on board survived the catastrophe.

Political obstinacy

The Russian Navy only confirmed the sinking of the *Kursk* two days after the incident, and

then initiated rescue operations, which were unsuccessful. After days of indecision, offers of support from Western countries, in particular England and the USA, were finally accepted. At the same time, fleet commanders hinted that the sinking was caused by a collision with a foreign submarine. Five days after the accident, Norwegian and British experts arrived on the scene of the disaster. On 21 August, deep-sea divers reached the wreck lying on the seabed about 100 m (328 ft) under the sea, and the deaths of the entire crew were officially confirmed.

The salvage operation

In October 2000, the Norwegian diving platform *Regalia* finally arrived at the site of the accident. Russian and Norwegian divers began salvage efforts. They were able to confirm that the two nuclear reactors that had been propelling the *Kursk* posed no further danger, as had been feared: diving robots found no evidence of heightened radioactivity near the

The farewell letter

Divers found a farewell note in the pocket of the uniform jacket worn by Captain Lieutenant Dmitri Kolesnikov. The note begins by stating that all 23 survivors have gathered in the ninth compartment of the boat.

Then Kolesnikov wrote: "Mustn't despair. It's too dark to write, but I'll try by touch. It seems there is no chance, no more than 10–20%. We hope that at least someone will read this."

Officers carrying the coffin of a dead officer of the Kursk. The funeral took place on 17 January 2001 in St. Petersburg, over a year after the catastrophe took place.

wreck. Working on the seabed, the salvage workers cut access holes in the submarine's hull to facilitate the search for bodies inside the boat. Norwegian divers, however, could only work on the outside of the wreck. For reasons of military secrecy, only Russian divers were permitted to go inside. After salvaging 12 bodies, work was halted. It was not until May 2001 that Moscow officially confirmed what Western experts had suspected all along: it was not a collision with a NATO submarine that caused the sinking of the *Kursk*, but the explosion of a torpedo inside the boat. A Dutch salvaging company was contracted to recover the wreck and towed it to a dock in Murmansk, where the bodies of more than 100 seamen were finally salvaged and laid to rest.

Grieving relatives visited the disaster area after it was officially confirmed that none of the crew survived the sinking of the Kursk.

2001

NINE-ELEVEN

THE 2001 TERRORIST ATTACKS ON THE USA

On September 11, 2001, four commercial airliners were hijacked on the east coast of the USA within a few minutes of each other. Within a little less than 20 minutes, two of the planes crashed into the twin towers of the World Trade Center in New York and a third hit the Pentagon, the US military head-quarters. The fourth plane did not strike its intended target, but crashed in a field in Pennsylvania. This series of catas-trophes claimed 3,056 lives, including the 19 hijackers, Islamic terrorists aiming a crushing blow against the symbols of Western democracies. Since this disaster, which has gone down in history as "Nine Eleven", the world is no longer what it used to be. The chasm between the fundamentalist states of the Middle East and the secular democracies of the Western world has become deeper.

A plane, United Airlines Flight 175, approached the south tower of the World Trade Center at 9:03 a. m. local time. Thick smoke was already pouring from the north tower, which had been hit moments earlier. The second plane hit the south tower, triggering an enormous explosion.

International Peace Day

On 7 September 2001, the United Nations General Assembly in New York passed a resolution that declared 21 September the annual International Day of Peace. Only four days later, the city of New York itself was the target of a terrorist attack on a scale that the world had until then deemed unthinkable. 11 September 2001 would become a symbol of horror, re-minding all the world's citizens that mindless terror may befall innocent, unsuspecting people at any time. "9–11" has become shorthand for the worst catastrophe of the very young twenty-first century. Is it mere coincidence that the very same sequence of numbers, 911, is also the nationwide emergency telephone number in the USA?

American Airlines Flight 11

At 7:59 a.m. local time, five terrorists boarded American Airlines Flight 11 in Boston. Their leader was Mohamed Atta, who had been living an apparently ordinary life as a university student in Hamburg, Germany for many years. He is a textbook example of a "sleeper", a covert operative who lives in a foreign environment as an unremarkable and law-abiding citizen until called to action. Only 30 minutes after take-off, flight attendant Betty Ong informed her airline's control centre that the plane was being hijacked. By 8:40 a.m. the terrorists, who had undergone pilot training in the USA specifically in preparation for this attack, were in control of the jet. The Boeing 767 took a turn and headed towards New York, descending to a lower altitude. Five minutes later, the plane crashed into the north tower of the World Trade Center, whose twin towers used to dominate New York's skyline. The plane crashed into the building on the 96th storey, penetrating into the centre of the tower. Some 40,000 litres (10,500 gallons) of fuel in the plane's almost full tank exploded, creating a fire of incredible intensity

The Pentagon was also a target of the terrorist attack. The collapsed section of the west wing is shown below.

The terrorists

On 27 September 2001, the US Department of Justice published a poster listing the alleged terrorists' names and photos. Eleven of the nineteen terrorists were from Saudi Arabia, the same country as terrorist mastermind Osama bin Laden.

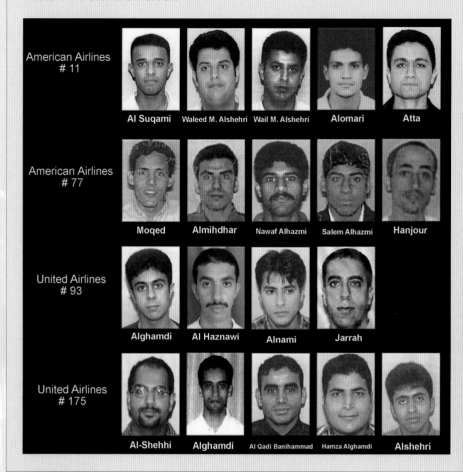

American Airlines # 11 — Al Suqami, Waleed M. Alshehri, Wail M. Alshehri, Alomari, Atta

American Airlines # 77 — Moqed, Almihdhar, Nawaf Alhazmi, Salem Alhazmi, Hanjour

United Airlines # 93 — Alghamdi, Al Haznawi, Alnami, Jarrah

United Airlines # 175 — Al-Shehhi, Alghamdi, Al Qadi Banihammad, Hamza Alghamdi, Alshehri

People crowded at the windows of the burning north tower of the World Trade Center in despair. There was little hope of saving them.

Jumpers

In the documentary film 9/11 by the brothers Jules and Gedeon Naudet, the sound of bodies thudding on the ground can be heard in the background again and again: people are jumping out of the windows of the burning World Trade Center in desparation. One of these jumpers landed on a firefighter, killing him. The exact number of jumpers who tried to escape death by suffocation or burning by this means is unknown; it is estimated that about 200 people died in this gruesome way. In consideration for the victims, the international media largely refrained from publishing such pictures. Only internet sites that specialize in publishing violent material – "snuff" videos – show these horrific pictures.

and temperatures of 1000 °C/1800 °F. The force of the plane's impact and the resulting explosion was so tremendous that part of the opposite side of the building was blown out. With all downward-leading escape routes completely destroyed, there was no hope of rescue for anyone who was located on the 96th floor or higher.

United Airlines Flight 175

Only 15 minutes after the first aircraft, the next hijacked plane took off from Boston's Logan International Airport. The Boeing jet, United Airlines Flight 175, was standing in the take-off queue just a few hundred metres behind the American airlines plane with Atta and other terrorists on board. Immediately prior to take-off, Atta had made a call from his cell phone to

talk to another student from Hamburg, Marwan al-Shehhi, who was in charge of flying the second plane. The aircraft was carrying 56 passengers and nine crew members. Half an hour after take-off, the terrorists tried to force their way into the cockpit. In order to force the pilots to open the doors, they stabbed several flight attendants.

Meanwhile, the first aircraft crashed into the north tower of the World Trade Center. CNN almost immediately began to broadcast footage of the burning building. During the broadcast, stunned viewers all around the world watched, unbelieving, as a second aircraft approached the towers, took a sharp turn and flew into the (until that point) undamaged south tower at 9:03 a.m. The pilot of this plane is presumed to be al-Shehhi.

Panic in New York

Live footage of the catastrophe was viewed by millions of people around the globe, and the entire world watched in horror and amazement. The towers were ablaze. All fire-fighting and ambulance units in New York were called to the scene and despite the chaos tried to evacuate the buildings and make their way to the upper storeys. Some of the people who found themselves on the floors above the points of impact even jumped to certain death in their desperation, hoping to escape the agony of death by suffocation or burning.

Meanwhile, the US government had begun to grasp the scope of the threat and addressed the possibility of further hijacked aircraft above American cities. At this point in time, about 2,200 planes were airborne in US airspace. All

The World Trade Center collapses in a massive cloud of dust and debris. The catastrophe was witnessed on TV by millions all over the world.

79

of those aircraft received instructions to divert immediately to the nearest airport. Interceptors took off in order to shoot down any aeroplanes that did not follow these instructions. As people around the world sat before their TVs in shock, the horrific scale of the New York catastrophe became increasingly apparent. At 9:59 a.m., the south tower collapsed and grey clouds of dust billowed through the canyons between skyscrapers. People in panic ran for their lives in the streets. The north tower, which had been hit a few minutes earlier than the south tower but higher up, withstood the fires half an hour longer. Then, at 10:28 a.m., it too collapsed. The steel frame construction near the point of impact was too weakened by the destructive force of the impact and the ensuing fires to carry the weight of the upper storeys. The

floors below were crushed as if by an avalanche. In total, 2,823 people died in this catastrophe, among them 343 rescue workers, who gave their lives to help others.

American Airlines Flight 77

While the images of the New York catastrophe were spreading around the world, two further death planes were already airborne. With five additional terrorists on board, American Airlines Flight 77 took off from Dulles International Airport just outside Washington, D.C. at 8:21 a.m. Its scheduled destination was Los Angeles on the West Coast of the USA. With the interceptors already airborne, American Airlines Flight 77 had been brought under the terrorists' control and turned around to head towards the US military headquarters. Around

Exhaustion and horror are written on the faces of these fire fighters sitting on the ruins of what used to be the World Trade Center.

9:40 a.m., the aircraft, with 53 passengers and six crew on board, crashed into the west wing of the Pentagon, a section that had recently been renovated and contained the Naval Command Center. The interceptors were too late to avert further tragedy: 125 military and government officials died in the building.

United Airlines Flight 93

By the time the fourth of the planes involved in the terrorist attacks took off from Newark, New Jersey at 8:42 a.m., after considerable delay, Mohamed Atta, leader of the terrorist group, was close to completion of the plan to crash into the WTC. There were four terrorists on board United Airlines Flight 93; their leader, Ziad Jarrah, was the third member of the Hamburg terrorist cell. After studying in Hamburg, he too took a short pilot training course in the USA. By 9:28 a.m. the terrorists were in control of the Boeing 757. The few passengers on board this aircraft managed to contact friends and relatives by phone, and thus learned about the events taking place in New York only a few minutes after their plane was taken over by the terrorists. The passengers instantly realized that a similar fate awaited them, too. The greater number of phone calls made from this plane has allowed experts to gain a clearer picture of

A crowd of rescue workers stands aghast amidst the ruins of the collapsed twin towers.

The attacks on Madrid's Atocha train station
At 7:30 a.m. on 11 March 2004, during morning rush hour, seven bombs placed in four commuter trains in Madrid's Atocha train station exploded. Three further bombs in the station could be deactivated in time; one of them would have been strong enough to destroy the entire building. Altogether, 191 people died and almost 2,000 were injured in the worst terrorist attack in Spanish history to date. The Spanish government initially suspected the Basque terrorist organization ETA, but soon discovered that the perpetrators were members of a local group of radical Muslims – not members of Al Qaeda, but inspired by Al Qaeda messages posted on the internet that advocated terrorism. A later attempt to arrest the terrorists ended with seven blowing themselves up, killing a police officer in the process.

what took place, and clearly, some of the passengers, facing certain death, decided to defeat the terrorists. Shortly before 10:00 a.m. a shout was heard – "Let's roll!" – the call for the determined passengers to subdue the hijackers.

The cockpit voice recorder found later captured sounds of the passengers' attempt to overwhelm the terrorists, who seem to be in distress. One of them shouted to the pilot, "Pull it down! Pull it down!" just before the aircraft ploughed into a field near Shanksville, Pennsylvania. There were no survivors. It remains unclear what this fourth plane's intended target was. Monuments of symbolic importance that were in the aircraft's path include the White House and the Capitol in Washington D.C., as well as Camp David.

Ground Zero
After 11 September 2001, the term "Ground Zero" became synonymous with the site of the New York catastrophe. The term originated back in the time of nuclear weapons tests and refers to the point of most severe destruction, the site of a nuclear bomb detonation. The World Trade Center, the US economy's central nervous system, was nothing more than a pile of rubble after the attack. Clean-up operations took almost a year, and the planning process for future use of the area took even longer. As of April 2006, construction work at this particularly valuable area in the middle of Manhattan had still not begun. There were architectural competitions, and there are specific plans for a "Freedom Tower", but the funding of this enormous project is not secure. Finally, the many victims' surviving dependants are making legitimate claims for a memorial site in remembrance of the catastrophe that shook America. The terror and fear associated with Nine Eleven and Ground Zero run deep: to this day, more than half of all New Yorkers would refuse to work at this place of horror.

New York firefighters amidst the debris that used to be the World Trade Center. In the course of rescue efforts, 343 firefighters lost their lives.

The London bombings

On 7 July 2005 Islamic terror reached the capital of the UK: London's public transport system fell victim to terrorist bombings. Around 8:30 a. m. public transport security cameras in London captured four men hugging each other euphorically. Later, it turned out that these men were carrying bombs in their backpacks, which were detonated soon afterwards: 20 minutes later, three bombs exploded in underground trains, and a fourth destroyed a bus about an hour later. In all, 56 people died and over 700 were injured. Initially it was unclear whether the attack was carried out by suicide bombers or whether timed detonators had been used. Later it emerged that the four terrorists were among the dead. Three were young men of Pakistani origin and the fourth came from Jamaica, but all four were British citizens and had lived completely inconspicuous lives in Leeds before the attacks. Not even their closest relatives knew of their radical potential and readiness to use violence.

WIPED OUT BY A MONSTER WAVE

THE SUMATRA TSUNAMI

Literally translated, the Japanese word *tsunami* means "harbour wave". These calamatous phenomena are triggered by an earthquake at sea, spreading in rings from the quake's epicentre and reaching heights of more than 30 m (98 ft). On 26 December 2004 at 7:58 a.m. local time, a seaquake of category 9.0 on the Richter scale shook the Indian Ocean off the north west coast of Sumatra. Due to its special characteristics, it triggered a flood wave that struck the coastal regions of Indonesia, Thailand, Sri Lanka and even East Africa, causing devastating damage. More than 230,000 people lost their lives in this terrible disaster.

The tsunami's third and largest wave surged over the promenade of Ao Nag Beach in Thailand.

A deadly wall of water crashes on land

It is in the Indian Ocean off the coast of Sumatra that the Indo-Australian and Eurasian continental plates lie alongside one another, and subterranean movement of the plates generates intense pressure and friction. This has always made the western coastal region of Indonesia an area prone to earthquakes. Within a rupture zone of about 1,000 km (600 miles), the Indio-Australian continental plate slides under the Eurasian plate by 7 cm (2¾ in) a year. This is not a slow, constant build-up of pressure, but happens suddenly with a jolt. Every jolt of this kind is registered as an earthquake by seismographs and recorded.

In the morning of 26 December 2004, a fateful disaster occurred in the Indian Ocean as about 500 km (300 miles) of sea floor broke open. Within seconds, unable to withstand the pressure created by the constant friction of the continental plates any longer, the tectonic plates thrust themselves between 10 and 30 m (30–100 ft) upwards, releasing energy of unimaginable magnitude. The underwater earthquake reached 9.0 on the Richter scale, making it the third most powerful earthquake ever recorded. The energy released is the equivalent of the total energy consumption of the USA for a whole year. However, this energy was not released at a single spot, as happens with an atomic bomb, for example. It was spread over a wide area, as an immense surface rose within seconds and pushed the water upwards. This created a wave whose height varied with the local water depth – the deeper the water, the higher the wave. The sea off the coast of Sumatra is about 5,000 m (16,500 ft) deep, and the flood wave generated on 26 December 2004 attained enormous height and sped towards the shore at almost 700 km/450 miles per hour, equivalent to the cruising speed of a plane.

On 2 January 2005, rescuers were still finding tsunami victims in a river in Banda Aceh, in northern Sumatra. The water retreated very slowly, revealing the full extent of the destruction.

Eyewitness report

"We felt a blow as if the boat had run aground at high speed or rammed a massive piece of driftwood or a wreck. A few seconds later, the boat was hit by a second blow and around 8:01 a. m. by a third. The instruments went haywire, the data on the GPS navigator was chaotic, and the plotter, sonar and radio were all dead. About ten minutes after the first hit, it seemed to us that the sea level had sunk by 10 or 15 metres. Without a sound and over a huge area the water simply sank away. Then we caught sight of gigantic waves on the south west horizon that reached the boat around 8:14 a. m. Seconds later, the boat, submerged in water up to the railing, was lifted up 30 metres. Three of these waves hit the boat all together, lifting it 50 metres above the previous height, that is, 35 metres above the normal water level."

Sofyan Anziba, captain of the fishing boat *Bintang Purnama*, which was at sea on the Straits of Malacca on 26 December 2004.

The Wave of Death was hardly noticed on the open sea; the sea level rose only slightly. It only became dangerous in shallower water as the wave approached the coast. Its speed was reduced, and the nearer the wave came to land the higher it piled up until it became a giant, deadly wall of water that crashed onto the shore, tearing up and engulfing everything in its path.

The appalling aftermath

The tsunami caused devastating destruction along the Bay of Bengal, the Andaman Sea and the west coasts of the Indian Ocean, even reaching Somalia on the East African coast 5,200 km (3,200 miles) away. It claimed more than 230,000 lives in eight Asian countries, among which Indonesia alone was left mourning 170,000 victims. Hundreds of thousands were injured, and 1,700,000,000 people lost their homes. The true number of victims is presumably much higher, since many regions beyond the tourist areas are practically unmapped. In addition, fear of disease led to mass burials and the cremation of corpses, making an accurate body count impossible. The immediate

A couple whose lives have been left in ruins by the terrible tsunami. Countless people lost literally everything they had.

In Banda Aceh alone, there were many more victims than originally thought. 122,000 are counted as dead and 114,000 as missing.

fear of disease and epidemics spread everywhere, as almost all sources of drinking water in the afflicted regions were contaminated. As a result of the hot climate and the many corpses, which were often only discovered and retrieved many days later, mosquitoes multiplied in masses and the outbreak of epidemic diseases such as cholera and typhus was feared likely. In India, the populace is inoculated against both, but these diseases were not the only anxiety. Contaminated water that infiltrates the respiratory tract can cause lung infections. Blood poisoning posed another widespread danger, as it can easily occur when wounds are exposed to dirty water. The humid climate, with temperatures continuously around 30 °C/86 °F, coupled with inadequate hygiene, is obviously highly conducive to such conditions.

Aftershocks shook the region

During the remaining days of 2004, the region experienced an average of 25 aftershocks a day, typically reaching a magnitude of 5.5 on the Richter scale.

On 28 March 2005, a quake of 8.7 magnitude, the last severe aftershock for the time being, rattled the west coast of Sumatra. It affected the Banyak Islands, Nias and Simeulue. As a result, 80 per cent of the buildings on Nias collapsed, and fatalities are estimated at around 2,000. Additional thousands of people were made homeless by this renewed assault.

**Eyewitness report
from Sri Lanka**
"All of a sudden, I found myself being swept out to sea with startling speed. Although I am a fairly strong swimmer, I was unable to withstand the current ... I swam in the direction of a loose catamaran, grabbed the hull and pulled myself to safety. My weight must have slowed the boat down, and soon I was stranded on the sand ... As the water rushed out of the bay, I scrambled onto the main road. Screams were coming from the houses beyond the road, many of which were still half full of water that had trapped the inhabitants inside. Villagers were walking, stunned, along the road, unable to comprehend what had taken place.

I was worried about my wife, who was on the beach when I went for my swim. I eventually found her walking along the road, dazed but happy to be alive. She had been trying to wade back to our island when the water carried her across the road and into someone's back yard. At one point she was underwater, struggling for breath. She finally grabbed onto a rope and climbed into a tree, escaping the waters that raged beneath her. Our children were still asleep when the tsunami struck at 9:15. They woke up to find the bay practically drained of water and their parents walking back across the narrow channel to safety."

Michael Dobbs, journalist
for the *Washington Post*,
27 December 2004

Geological after-effects, economic and cultural damage

As a geological after-effect, 15 of the 572 islands that comprise the Andaman and Nicobar Islands, situated in the Indian Ocean to the south east of the Bay of Bengal, sank below sea level. In addition, both the Nicobar Islands and the Island of Simeulue that lies off the coast of

Nothing is left of the exclusive Laguna resort in Khao Lag (southern Thailand) but a pile of rubble.

In April 2005, under a psychologist's supervision, children were sent onto the beach to try and overcome their trauma.

Sumatra and is nearest to the epicentre of the quake, have shifted approximately 15 m (50 ft) to the south west.

Apart from the human tragedies, the tsunami also caused enormous cultural and ecological damage. For example, approximately 10 per cent of the coral reefs off the coast of Thailand were either damaged or eradicated. It will take decades for this natural protection from high waves to recover to its pre-2004 condition.

Further natural coastal protection is provided by the mangrove swamps, which were also destroyed by the flood wave. The native fauna was also badly affected. On the island of Nicarugo, for example, the last living turtles of a rare species were killed, and the nesting areas of the Leatherback and Sea Turtles were badly disrupted. The humus has been washed away by the mass of water that hit the land with such great force and only retreated after some time; the areas affected have thus become relatively barren. Along coastal strips between 250 m and 3 km (800 ft–2 miles) in width, the fertile soil layer, often no deeper than 30 cm (12 in), has been washed away and the plants ripped out. The harvests of the coming years therefore can be expected to be extremely poor. In several regions, historic buildings such as museums and historic monuments have been completely obliterated. According to UNESCO, treasures belonging to the world's cultural heritage are in ruins, including the Old Town and fortifications

Foreshocks and aftershocks: what does magnitude tell us about the energy released?
The magnitude of the foreshocks and aftershocks off the coast of Sumatra around 26 December 2004 ranged between 5.0 and 9.1 (the main quake) on the Richter scale. An increase of one point on the Richter scale entails a 32-fold increase in the energy released. The main earthquake with a magnitude of 9.1 therefore released 32 times more energy than an aftershock of a magnitude of 8.1. Compared to a quake of 5.1, the main earthquake released 1,048,576 times more energy.

Natural phenomenon tsunami: FAQs

WHAT CAUSES A TSUNAMI?
Tsunamis are most often caused by underwater earthquakes or volcanic eruptions. However, they can also be caused by a meteorite impact.

WHERE ARE TSUNAMIS MOST FREQUENT?
Around 90 per cent occur in the Pacific Ocean and in south east Asia, though they can also occur elsewhere. Following the Lisbon earthquake of 1755, for example, 60,000 people were killed by a tidal wave that swallowed up everything along the course of the River Tejo, thus doing due justice to its name of "harbour wave".

HOW HIGH CAN A TSUNAMI GET?
An earthquake off the coast of Alaska in 1964 triggered a monster wave that reached a height 30 m (100 ft) when it struck Hilo, Hawaii's largest city. When Krakatoa erupted in 1883, a wave of 40 m (130 ft) engulfed coastal regions. It is said that a tidal wave off the Japanese island of Ishigaki reached a height of 85 m (280 ft) in 1971. When tsunamis force their way into narrow bays or fjords (such as the mouth of the Tejo in Lisbon) they can grow much higher. According to folklore, the eruption at Santorini over 3,000 years ago is said to have triggered a wave of 250 m (800 ft).

In all this, it should be remembered that a tsunami is not a mass of flowing water like a river. Rather, it is a transfer of energy in which one water molecule hits the next and so on. The deeper the sea where the wave is triggered, the higher the wall of water becomes when it reaches land.

HOW FAR CAN A TSUNAMI WAVE TRAVEL?
A tsunami can travel halfway around the globe. The tidal wave of the 1964 quake off Alaska caused considerable damage in New Zealand. Tsunamis can easily travel more than 10,000 km (6,000 miles) without losing force.

WHAT SPEED CAN A TSUNAMI REACH?
Here, too, water depth is the decisive factor. Speeds of up to 1,000 km/600 miles per hour are not unusual. At this speed, it takes no longer than a day for a wave to reach every conceivable point in the Pacific region.

WHICH TSUNAMI CAUSED THE GREATEST DAMAGE AND INFLICTED THE GREATEST LOSS OF LIFE TO DATE?
The tragic record in both is held by the Sumatra tsunami of 2004, followed by the Alaskan tsunami of 1964, the tsunami following the 1896 Sanriku earthquake in Japan, and the monster wave caused by the Krakatoa eruption of 1883.

of Galle in Sri Lanka, the ancient monuments at Mahabalipuram in India and the Sun Temple of Konarak.

Tourism has inevitably suffered, as many tourists avoid places that have been visited by such disasters. As a result, the surviving inhabitants who had depended on tourism for their livelihood become poorer still. Women in particular struggle with the social aftermath of the disaster. In many of the affected regions, a woman cannot marry if there is no dowry for her. Many young women therefore suffer, disgraced by their poverty, and suicide rates amongst young women in some areas have escalated.

How to measure the magnitude of a disaster?

In an age replete with disasters, every calamity becomes the "greatest disaster of the century"

or even the "greatest disaster of the age". Such superlatives are not always appropriate. It is true that the extent of the area affected by the Sumatra tsunami is unequaled in history. Also unparalleled is the fact that, owing to mass tourism, the victims included people from almost every country in the world. There are other disasters, however, either restricted to a particular region or occurring in countries intolerant of politically negative media attention, that claim yet more lives than the tsunami of 2004. China, for example, has regularly suffered from devastating floods such as the one in the Henan province in 1887 that took more than 900,000 lives. At the other extreme, the disastrous drought in India between 1965 and 1967 claimed the lives of some 1,500,000,000 people. The question of how to measure the magnitude of a disaster must remain a matter of debate.

Arial photography gives an impression of the devastation in Sumatra in the wake of the 2004 tsunami.

2005

A STORM'S TERRIFYING TRAIL OF DESTRUCTION

KATRINA: ONE OF THE WORLD'S DEADLIEST HURRICANES

Between 25 and 31 August 2005, Hurricane Katrina first hit the south east coast and then the south coast of the United States. Growing from a category 3 to a category 5 hurricane, it laid waste to the entire infrastructure of about 200 km (125 miles) of coastline, destroying everything in its path and changing the face of one of America's most distinctive cities, New Orleans, forever. Katrina proved to be one of the most devastating hurricanes of all time.

This car park in Fort Lauderdale, north of Miami, Florida, was hit by Katrina on 25 August 2005. The immense force of the hurricane is clearly visible.

Hurtling energy over the Gulf of Mexico

With wind gusts of 130 km/80 miles per hour, a hurricane newly dubbed Katrina struck the densely inhabited south east coast of Florida on 25 August 2005. Though it was "only" a category 1 hurricane at the time, it caused substantial property damage and several people lost their lives. Damage attributed to the flooding caused by the heavy rainfall accompanying the

storm ran into millions of dollars. The population along the south coast, so often plagued by hurricanes, breathed a sigh of relief as Katrina turned away and moved over the Gulf of Mexico.

Unfortunately, this was premature. By late summer the waters of the gulf had warmed to about 30 °C/86 °F, and fuelled by this heat from below Katrina gained enormously in strength and especially in size. Within a short time it grew to become a category 5 hurricane with top wind speeds of more than 250 km/155 miles per hour. It also changed direction again and began to approach America's south coast. A mandatory evacuation of the 480,000 inhabitants of the city of New Orleans was issued on 28 August. People barricaded their houses, nailing planks and boards over doors and windows before moving to safety (often against their will). Yet tens of thousands of the city's inhabitants slipped through the law's net and remained in their city.

On 29 August Katrina hit southern Louisiana and Mississippi with stunning force, devastating a coastal strip almost 200 km (125 miles) wide. The destruction was so extensive that the entire infrastructure was demolished. Hurri-

canes lose strength relatively quickly over land, however, and, luckily for New Orleans, Katrina hit the city as a category 3 hurricane with winds of "only" 200 km/125 miles per hour. The damage it wreaked was nevertheless immense. Whole sections of New Orleans were razed and almost the entire city was flooded after a series of critical levies were breached. Katrina weakened to a tropical storm over the state of Mississippi, and continued to lose strength as it made its way through Alabama, Tennessee, Kentucky and Ohio. Fortunately, although accompanied by heavy rainfall and the occasional tornado, Katrina had lost much of its enormous destructive force, and its journey finally ended on 31 August.

The devastating aftermath

During this natural disaster, which plunged the United States into a deep domestic political crisis, more than 1,500 people lost their lives. Thousands were still missing months afterwards. Millions were homeless for many days and weeks, and even today, many are still unable to return to their homes. Whole suburbs of New Orleans lie in ruins and may never be restored to their former glory. Almost one year

Long queues of people waited for buses to transport them to the Astrodome in Houston, Texas, outside of the danger zone.

The Saffir-Simpson hurricane scale

Category 1: 119–153 km/74–95 miles per hour
Category 2: 154–177 km/96–110 miles per hour
Category 3: 178–209 km/111–130 miles per hour
Category 4: 210–249 km/131–155 miles per hour
Category 5: over 250 km/156 miles per hour

Only three other hurricanes prior to Katrina have reached category 5:
Andrew, 1992, Florida, 43 dead
Camille, 1969, Mississippi, 256 dead
nameless, 1935, Florida, 600 dead

The 7th Ward in New Orleans was hit especially hard by Katrina. Aid workers had great difficulty controlling the situation.

after Katrina, some 100,000 people in Mississippi and the neighbouring state of Louisiana continue to live in caravans instead of houses, because their homes are still uninhabitable. Many thousands more have left for other parts of the country and may never return. The immediate damage caused by the tragedy amounted to $150 billion, while the medium- and long-term damage is estimated at more than $600 billion. This almost unimaginable sum makes Katrina the most destructive hurri-

cane of all time; in terms of material loss, its wreckage exceeds even that of the Indian Ocean tsunami disaster in late 2004 (see page 84). Katrina has therefore achieved the tragic record of being the world's worst natural disaster, and one of the three deadliest hurricanes in the history of the United States. We can be extremely grateful that it did not claim the same unspeakably high toll in human life as the 2004 tsunami and other disasters, but primarily caused material damage.

Emergency shelter for the inhabitants of the city's poorest districts was provided in the New Orleans Convention Center.

Post-disaster chaos

The tally immediately after Katrina showed that almost one million people had lost their homes and at least 350,000 houses had been rendered uninhabitable. The City of New Orleans, which lies at or below sea level and is thus highly prone to flooding, was under water, in places as much as 6 m (20 ft) deep. Days after the disaster, the supply situation remained chaotic and people were still waiting on rooftops to be rescued. There was a shortage of drinking water, the water supply was cut off, there was no food, no electricity and no telephone service.

Prior to 25 August, New Orleans held the dismal record of being the city with the second highest rate of murder and violent crime in America (no. 1 is Camden, New Jersey). Looting began soon after the hurricane subsided, with people carrying off anything of value they could find. Violence escalated. One looter even gunned down a police officer standing in his way. Martial law was declared in the city, and still thousands of national guard troops and police officers were unable to stem the violence that broke out in the aftermath of Katrina. Even aid and rescue operations had to be halted in some cases. As a result, tens of thousands of people were trapped in New Orleans for days without medical care. Corpses drifted through the flood waters, toxic substances leaked into the water, and an unbearable stench hovered over the city. The threat of disease was acute. In addition to all the damage on land, US coastguards announce that 20 oil platforms were missing in the Gulf of Mexico.

After several days, food, drinking water and medical supplies finally began to reach the people in the city. President George W. Bush admitted that he had failed to assess the situation adequately and made $60 billion in aid available. His first response had cost far less: he had asked Americans to pray for their suffering fellow citizens.

Criticism of preparations for the emergency

It was the breach of the levies of the higher-lying Lake Pontchartrain that flooded the city with water until it reached the same level as the lake. Today, many American experts criticize the government for taking inadequate precautions in the 1960s against a possible disaster; they had prepared for far less powerful storms than Katrina.

Recent studies show that when planning the levies to protect New Orleans, the worst pos-

---

Hurricanes

The average hurricane has a diameter of 550 km (340 miles) and releases more energy in one day than all the power plants on earth combined. In 2005, all previous world records for measured hurricanes were broken. In that year, Wilma and Katrina became the strongest storms ever measured. But it was not only in the USA that such storms occurred. In Asia, fierce typhoons (the local name for hurricanes) also raged in 2005. Europe has been spared such storms up to now, because European waters do not have the necessary surface temperatures for the creation of hurricanes. However, scientists warn that warming of the Mediterranean could in the future lead to the formation of hurricanes in Europe, too.

The strongest hurricanes since 1900:
1900: USA – Galveston
1935: USA – Labor Day Hurricane
1961: Central America – Hattie

1969: USA – Camille
1979: Japan – Tip
1988: Caribbean – Gilbert
1992: USA – Andrew
1996: Taiwan and China – Herb
1998: Caribbean – Mitch
2000: China – Saomai
2001: Taiwan – Nari
2004: Japan – Tokage
2004: Grenada, Jamaica, Cuba and USA – Ivan
2005: Cuba and USA – Dennis, Katrina and Rita
2005: Central America – Stan
2005: Mexico and USA – Wilma
2005: Azores, Canary Islands and Spain – Vince
2005: Taiwan – Haitang
2005: China – Matsa, Talim, Khanun and Damrey
2005: China and Taiwan – Longwang
2005: Japan – Nabi

The damage caused by Hurricane Katrina was immense. Little of this McDonald's in Biloxi, Mississippi was left standing apart from Ronald.

Eyewitness report

"It was one of the most awesome experiences of my life, as I was in New Orleans at the end of 2005. I was overwhelmed on several levels. Everywhere, I found strange scenes and bizarre objects – overturned automobiles resting on roofs, boats in living rooms. Whole precincts of the city looked as if they had been bombed, toilets and beds and dishes lay everywhere in ironic and biting contradiction. I could have shot a series on the unbelievable force of nature alone, but I had traveled there to occupy myself with something other than just the destruction. It took a quite a lot of discipline to remain true to my intention and concentrate on the more subtle signs of human tragedy. I experienced a deep feeling of mourning and loss there; not commiseration for the damage and loss the victims have suffered, but much more a feeling for that which was happening to me myself, the feeling everyone suffers when a disaster of this immensity hits his own countrymen. Over the past few years the USA has lost something holy, and Katrina is the visible evidence for this. It has to do with our community, with compassion and solidarity that has been sacrificed to our materialistic society. I, as a person, am willing to face up to this damage, and perhaps, through my work, I can persuade others to do likewise."

Chris Jordan, photographer, on the lasting consequences of Katrina

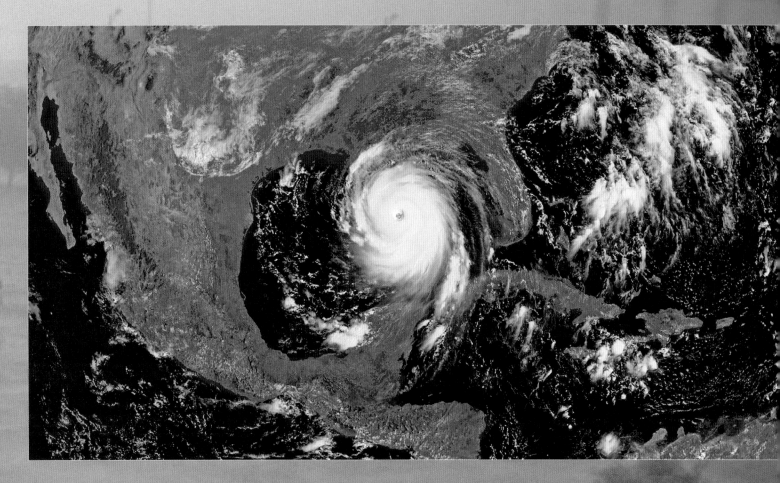

This satellite picture shows Katrina approaching the Gulf coast of Louisiana and Mississippi.

sible disaster had not been considered. Due to prohibitive cost, much weaker storms had been assumed, and the dimensions of the levies set accordingly. The engineers had simply not included the worst possible storm in their calculations. It should be asked, however: are we ever fully prepared for a disaster?

Global warming

Climatic researchers have demonstrated that global temperatures have risen and will continue to rise as a result of the greenhouse effect. First and foremost, it is the surface temperature of the seas that has risen by an average of 0.5 °C/0.9 °F. Hurricane research has shown that the surface temperature of the oceans plays one of the most significant roles in their physical creation. Enough water evaporates at a surface temperature of 26 °C/79 °F or more to generate and fuel a hurricane. But the warming of the air over the oceans is also decisive. The higher the air temperature rises, the greater the quantity of moisture it can absorb, and this results in increased energy and intensity of a hurricane. In Katrina's case, the high temperature of the water in the Gulf of Mexico is one of the factors that fed its energy and intensity until it reached the highest hurricane category.

As additional seas exceed the critical threshold of 26 °C/79 °F and become warmer, more and more hurricanes will develop. Some researchers also consider it likely that the future has hurricanes in store for the Mediterranean region. Not only has the number of tropical hurricanes increased over the last 20 years, but their intensity and duration are on the rise, as well.

Picture Credits